Mastering Fundamental Analysis

Mastering Fundamental Analysis

MICHAEL C. THOMSETT

Dearborn
Financial Publishing, Inc.®

This publication is designed to provide accurate and authoritative information in regard to the subject matter covered. It is sold with the understanding that the publisher is not engaged in rendering legal, accounting, or other professional service. If legal advice or other expert assistance is required, the services of a competent professional person should be sought.

Editorial Director: Cynthia A. Zigmund
Managing Editor: Jack Kiburz
Interior Design: Lucy Jenkins
Cover Design: S. Laird Jenkins Corporation

© 1998 by Michael Thomsett

Published by Dearborn Financial Publishing, Inc.®

Printed in the United States of America

99 00 10 9 8 7 6 5 4 3

Library of Congress Cataloging-in-Publication Data
Thomsett, Michael C.
    Mastering fundamental analysis : how to spot trends and pick winning stocks using fundamental analysis / Michael C. Thomsett.
        p.   cm.
    Includes index.
    ISBN 0-7931-2873-0
    1. Investment analysis. 2. Stocks—United States. 3. Stock exchanges—United States. I. Title.
    HG4529.T49   1998   98–8159
    332.63'22'0973—dc21   CIP

Dearborn books are available at special quantity discounts to use as premiums and sales promotions, or for use in corporate training programs. For more information, please call the Special Sales Manager at 800-621-9621, ext. 4384, or write to Dearborn Financial Publishing, Inc., 155 N. Wacker Drive, Chicago, IL 60606-1719.

CONTENTS

PREFACE

What This Book Will Do for You

As an investor, you want and need basic information to select a company whose stock will meet your investment goals. You need the fundamentals—information about a company that tells you about financial consistency and reliability, profits, dividends, property and debts, and other dollars-and-cents information.

Simple, straightforward information in a practical format is difficult to find. When you begin reading reports prepared by accountants and analysts you can lose your way easily, unless you are a financial expert yourself. If you depend on books for information on evaluating a company's fundamentals, you find that basic information is equally difficult to locate—until now.

This book is written for investors, not for financial experts. If you want to improve your skills at fundamental analysis, this book is for you. It leads you through researching and analyzing fundamental financial information in order to forecast profits, supply and demand, industry strength, management ability, and other factors affecting a stock's market value and growth potential.

To the extent that math is necessary to make a point in this book, we will explain the process step by step, provide examples, and walk you through the explanation. You want and need intelligent, practical advice to support your investment needs, and this book will address that need. We avoid stock market industry information controlled by analysts and accountants who express themselves in technical terms and use detailed statistical modeling to communicate with one another.

This book, written for the nonaccountant who wants basic investment information, teaches you to master the essentials of fundamental analysis. These include studying financial statements, interpreting trends, using ratios, and making informed decisions based on tangible information. This is possible without having to take a course in high-level accounting or statistical analysis. Certainly, there is a need for technical communication among financial professionals. However, that does not address *your* needs as an investor. The gap in market information occurs invariably in communication, between experts who have the information and nonexperts who need the information.

This basic, practical guide uses a series of tools to help break down technical ideas and concepts so that you can make practical use of the information. These tools include

- *worksheets and forms* you can use to compile information about companies and compare it;
- *graphs and charts* to express the ideas behind columns and rows of numbers in a way that makes sense to help visualize results;
- *checklists* of action ideas and points worth remembering;
- *examples* that clarify and illustrate important points;
- *definitions* placed in context so that ideas come across clearly, so you can overcome jargon used by technical experts;
- *key points* set aside and highlighted for ease of recognition; and
- *walk-throughs* to help with processes such as mathematical formulas.

Collectively, these tools will help you teach yourself the essential elements of fundamental analysis, but avoid the complexities often associated with finance. We all tend to resist new information, even when we need it. This book will help you overcome the resistance and achieve a mastery of the valuable tools you need to make informed decisions.

Nothing in the study of financial information is so complex that it cannot be grasped by the average investor. No topic is so technical that you cannot follow the concept, and there are no ideas that are available only to the technician. Those ideas and concepts will be explained simply and thoroughly so you can make use of them.

The Big Secret Is ... There Is No Big Secret

That there *is* no secret is the biggest secret of Wall Street—and of any specialized industry. Very little in the financial world is so complex that you cannot grasp it. The fundamentals are—as their name implies—fundamental, basic, uncomplicated. The only factor complicating financial information is jargon, overly complex statistical analysis, and complex formulas that don't convey information any better than straight talk.

For instance, the essential purpose of preparing financial reports is to clarify and communicate information. The basis of fundamental analysis is accounting, and accounting is little more than the reporting of transactions: where money and obligations come from and where they go. The best accounting systems are clear and simple, so it is easy to track the money. Accounting also is designed to help analysts spot trends and forecast likely outcomes based on those trends. This book deals mainly with the two primary purposes of financial reporting: simplicity in interpreting the numbers, and analysis based on those numbers.

With the vast amount of information available through publication of financial statements, analysts' reports, the financial press, and the Internet, a large part of the information-gathering task is already performed for you. The difficult thing for you as an investor is to decide which information to use. Not all of the vast array of available data is reliable, relevant, or especially useful in making the decision to buy, hold, or sell a particular stock.

This book, first of all, assumes that all of the information investors need is readily available, that it can be understood completely if it is examined and explained properly, and that the real challenge for the investor is bridging the gap between finding information and applying to it the decision-making process. To a degree, analysis is already performed for you by services like Value Line and Standard & Poor's, not to mention the in-depth analysis going on constantly in the financial press. Second, the book is carefully designed to present information in a highly visual manner. This includes the emphasis of key points for ease of reference; generous use of graphs, charts, forms, and worksheets; plenty of examples; walk-throughs for mathematical procedures; and definitions provided when a term or phrase is first introduced. These tools and techniques make fundamental analysis practical for and readily available to you.

Unlike many investment programs that propose a specific method, we do not suggest that everyone will be comfortable with one approach. This book explains how each type of fundamental information works and what it shows; it is left to you to decide which technique should be given the greatest weight, or which should even be used at all. The basic assumption is that, as an individual, each investor wants to set up a program for maximum comfort and ease.

To be sure that the tests you decide to apply to information are valid and meaningful, this book suggests possible ways to approach the analysis of a stock, a portfolio, an industry, or a particular strategy. The intention is to give you the information to decide how to proceed, based on your personal strategy, risk tolerance, market attitude and philosophy, and personality. This book offers no magic formula, and *will not* show you how to "get rich quick" through fundamental analysis. It *will* show you how to "get informed quickly" in the belief that having good information leads to good decision making, and that decision makers are rewarded through success and profits.

CHAPTER 1

Defining the Fundamentals— What You Need

Most investors depend on financial information to judge companies. And why not? Dollars are how business keeps score, judges success, forecasts the future, and determines who is outperforming the competition. Fundamental analysis is the method of choice because it provides dependable, consistent information.

What can you expect from fundamental tests and why perform analysis at all? These questions are good starting points because they establish the very reasons to undertake analysis. Fundamental tests, more than anything else, provide a means for comparison. We can make judgments only by comparing one thing to another. We don't know what our preferences are until we look at two or more alternatives. This is as true in the stock market as it is everywhere else. Fundamental tests are a consistent application of standards to several companies. We hope the results of those tests will guide us in our decisions to select one stock over another; and then to buy, hold, or sell.

But why perform analysis at all? Why not simply choose stocks by throwing darts at the stock listings? Some people make an argument that random selection of stocks is as effective a method as any other. The *random walk* theory, for example, says stock prices change in a random and unpredictable manner, and that the effect of new information on market prices cannot be predicted with any degree of certainty.

Anyone who seriously approaches investing has to question the wisdom of the random walk theory. It just makes sense that studying

1

fundamental, intrinsic information about a company leads to an intelligent stock selection, while the failure to perform research may result in bad choices—a loss of money. Most people agree that doing research is better than *not* doing research.

A second theory concerning the market is the *efficient market* theory, which states that the current price of a stock reflects all known information about the company. The theory also states that as new information becomes known, it is factored into the stock's price immediately. This theory assumes that some group—presumably the market as a whole—keeps track of information and immediately raises or lowers its estimation of market value. In reality, most people know that the stock market has a degree of chaos to it, and that such efficiency is suspect and unlikely.

Two more likely reactions to new information are to completely discount the information, thus not affecting the stock's market price, or to temporarily overreact, greatly affecting the price.

It is easy to theorize about market forces, supply and demand, and the psychological nature of the typical investor—all without really knowing how the market works. Such is the nature of any theory. If it were possible to know precisely how the market works, it might be easier to know how to pick stocks. Because prices change, often without obvious cause and effect, a degree of excitement surrounds stock market investing. That excitement makes it easy to fall into belief systems that have no basis in fact. It is important to remember, though, that the market prices of stocks reflect a perception of value rather than a reaction to any new logical or fundamentally based information.

Defining Fundamental Analysis

Fundamental analysis is a method of research that studies basic financial information to forecast profits, supply and demand, industry strength, management ability, and other intrinsic matters affecting a stock's market value and growth potential. The resulting information can help you maintain perspective. Certainly some aspects of price movement in the stock market are beyond logic, and baffling to anyone with a logical mind. The fundamentals—those intrinsic *facts* about a company—can be used to forecast financial performance and, to some degree, stock price movements. More investors use fundamentals than other methods. Nonfundamental methods are collectively known as *technical analysis.* The dedicated technical analyst (or "technician") shuns fundamentals, often on the premise that financial reporting is merely historical, yesterday's old information, and by its very nature, of no use. Accordingly, such information has nothing to do with how a stock's market price will move tomorrow or the next day.

Both fundamental and technical analysis use trends, but in different ways. The fundamental approach employs historical information (dividend rates, profits, or sales, for example) to forecast financial results. Technicians use trends. Technical analysis is highly visual and largely ignores the basic premise of supply and demand, believing instead that recent price trends (shown as charts) dictate future price movement. Essential to the charting theory is the idea of *support level* and *resistance level.* These levels are derived from a study of a stock's recent price changes. When the price moves below the support level (the lowest expected price) or above the resistance level (the highest expected price), that is called a *breakout*; that is, a price movement outside the established range. The concepts of support and resistance levels and breakout are summarized in Figure 1.1.

Even those who swear by the fundamentals should recognize that technical analysis serves a useful purpose. But not even the most faithful of number crunchers can ignore that widespread belief in a fundamental indicator that can move market prices far above or below

FIGURE 1.1 Trading Range

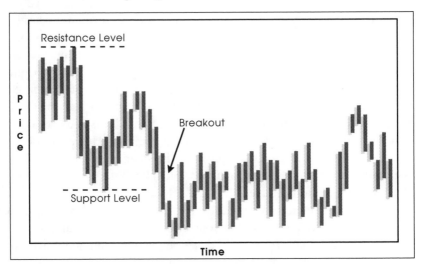

intrinsic values. Such technical analysis and the resulting indicators, however, are only short-term in nature. Fundamental analysis can be a valuable tool if used as research for long-term prospects, but not for tracking day-to-day stock price movement, market reaction to news or rumor, and temporary popularity of one industry group over another.

⋏ KEY POINT

Most of the financial news we get emphasizes short-term opinion and trends. Long-term information is more valuable but harder to come by.

Successful investors must consider the long term, and that is where fundamental analysis is valuable. Even the most serious investors tend to listen to current gossip and news, though they have no intention of abandoning a well-structured long-term strategy. The market is in many respects a huge gossip mill, and those involved in it love to whisper and spread stories and rumors. Such behavior is emotional, not rational. This is important to keep in mind when attempting to place some logical value on most of the news you hear.

As a believer in fundamental analysis and its value, you must believe that you can make decisions in a rational, logical manner. If you have a strong bias against or for a particular company or industry, the value of fundamental analysis is already compromised. Information should be given the appropriate consideration based on its merits, without regard for the bias that we all bring to the process. Avoiding our biases is a valuable practice and not necessarily an easy one. You may begin by setting as a rule that you are seeking valid information, not attempting to confirm a bias. Otherwise, any form of research is a waste of time. You may as well invest based on preconceived ideas and take your chances in the market, which is not at all uncommon. However, a bias is likely to impede success (i.e., profit) rather than add to it. So a first assumption about fundamental analysis has to be that if you will use it, you need to remain objective.

A second assumption, of equal importance, must be that you can analyze and research as well as anyone else. You have no doubt experienced an attitude that professionals such as mutual fund and portfolio managers have more information than the rest of us, and that they know how to beat the averages. This attitude is promoted primarily by professionals. In fact, in one extensive study, only about 22 percent beat "average."[*]

🔑 KEY POINT

Professionals don't do any better than the rest of us in beating the market over time. You have just as much of a chance at success if you perform your own research.

Also remember that the main emphasis in the financial news is on short-term thinking, but that is not where the profits are to be made. Experts like to predict where the Dow Jones Industrials will be in six months or a year—but this provides no valuable information to serious investors.

🔑 KEY POINT

Long-term investing in the stock market produces profits. Short-term predictions may be interesting today, but they are of no informational value for long-term portfolio decisions.

To begin looking at fundamental analysis as a tool for getting useful information, you must recognize the limitations of short-term fads, predictions, and odds-beating games; and accept the premise that the market rewards investors over time. This reward is why the stock

---

[*] Survey by *Consumer Reports,* in 1985, of 289 mutual funds. The study looked at performance measured against the market between 1980 and 1984, and found that only 63 funds beat the market (measured by the S&P 500).

In a more recent Morningstar Inc. survey of diversified stock funds cited in *The New York Times*, January 11, 1998, the majority fell short even in the bull markets between 1994 and 1997. Only 24 percent of such funds beat the market in 1994; 16 percent in 1995; 26 percent in 1996; and only 10 percent in 1997.

market is popular. Successful shareholders make the most money when they leave their investment capital in the market. Betting on the short term, following the crowd and its herd mentality, and listening to pundits who are only guessing, will never take the place of a sound, long-term strategy for rational, intelligent study and research.

You may ask, if short-term guessing is proven to be of no value, and if professionals consistently fail to beat the market average, then what good does it do to study financial statements? In other words, what do yesterday's results tell us about investments that will be "good" or "bad" tomorrow?

The answer is not a question of whether you will make a profit within a few weeks of buying 100 shares of stock; that is short-term thinking. Any stockbroker can readily list 10 or 20 well-managed blue chip companies whose long-term prospects are excellent, whose stock will probably rise, and whose dividend payments will no doubt remain competitive. The real value of fundamental analysis is comparative in narrowing the list of possible investments. By comparing financial information among several corporations, you can judge relative value, and make your own judgment about potential profits.

Many investors choose mutual funds because you can then invest in a number of companies or industries. Only with a vast sum of pooled capital can you invest in all of the companies you like, and thus achieve the advantage of diversification at the same time.

When you have identified a number of "good" choices—well-managed companies in strong competitive positions, with plenty of capital, good management, a long-standing reputation, and other market strengths—you may question the value in performing the analysis at all. Why not simply pick one of those well-rated companies? This is, by the way, precisely the method used by thousands of investors.

One of the principal advantages of studying the numbers is that it enables you to identify stocks that are currently undervalued by the market, those that may represent a buying opportunity with long-term potential. On the other hand, if you own stocks that are overvalued by the market, that may be a signal that it's time to sell.

These criteria may sound like short-term judgment calls, but remember that long-term decisions ultimately consist of monitoring and acting on short-term information. At some point, a long-held stock wears out its promise and becomes less attractive. With fundamental analysis, you can monitor your portfolio to know when to sell or hold. The decision to buy is often given great emphasis, but it represents only the first step in maintaining your portfolio. To succeed as an investor, you don't want to make any decisions haphazardly, including the decision to do nothing. Investors must monitor their portfolios constantly, so they can know if and when yesterday's strategies no longer apply.

Example: You purchased 300 shares of stock in a promising new technology company nearly ten years ago. At the time, the stock was selling for $1.25 per share. The stock has been valued at $15 per share for more than a year. The latest annual report seems to suggest that the company has reached a threshold in terms of size—number of employees, annual sales, profits—that it is unable to exceed. The various techniques you employ in watching fundamental trends tells you that this investment has topped out.

In this example, you were able to change a "hold" decision—the default position—to a "sell" decision based on trend analysis. The topping out effect—common for companies that are through growing—is not a negative in the same respect that net losses or loss of position in an industry would be. It is simply a sign that you have gotten all you can expect from that particular investment. The example applies not only to small stocks in initial growth phases, but equally well to large companies with long standing in the market, such as IBM or Navistar.

Rates of growth, degree of expansion, and capital limitations are some of the variables in fundamental analysis. You can judge these matters only by comparing companies' current and past financial records. This is where the intrinsic value of fundamental analysis outshines any technical indicators. Numbers do not lie. If a trend slows, stops, and reverses itself, the numbers are reflecting exactly what happened in recent weeks or months. Don't become caught up in the popular notion that the near future can be predicted by index levels or popular stocks. Only by performing focused fundamental analyses of real financial results is it possible to see short-term as well as long-term trends.

We tend to think of financial information as being scientific and pure. Based on the numbers alone, a case could be made that fundamental analysis is the science of market research. Unfortunately, fundamental analysis cannot be given a complete bill of health because the human element enters the picture. The professional analyst tends to make the waters murky in the same way that trendy analysis clouds the issue of current market health.

Example: One company has earned more than 9 percent net profit during the past three years, even though it only forecast an 8 percent annual profit. In the most recently ended year, the analysts predicted another 9 percent return; however, actual results came out at 8 percent.

This all too common example makes a point about the flaw in the use of fundamental analysis. Humans cannot resist the urge to make predictions. The 8 percent return, because it is lower than the expert forecast, would be seen as a negative and a short-term reduction in market value would result—even though the actual rate of net return is excellent.

✒ KEY POINT

Positive or negative predictions are reflections of market perception rather than of real financial facts.

A company's stock rises or falls on a report that is at variance with a prediction. What is lost in all of this is the real meaning of the results. If a company can be reasonably expected to net 8 percent and the analysts predict 10 percent, then a 9 percent return will probably cause a negative reaction. Remember, the market reacts illogically, almost always overreacting to news.

✒ KEY POINT

The tendency of the market to overreact gives you a great advantage. By adhering to the fundamentals and resisting the temptation to follow short-term trends, you are able to keep your head while others do not.

The analysts may see the example as a disappointing result compared to the past, and issue a negative report. The market would react negatively as well. In the minds of the analyst, less is always worse, and more is always better. In the real world, one needs to take a close look at real results in real markets.

Measuring the Market

Many people measure the market's rise and fall using the all-popular Dow Jones Industrial Average (DJIA), which includes a mere 30 companies. Most people, including experts, watch the DJIA because they believe it sets a trend for the market. Be aware that the index does not measure the mood, but defines it.

Some background: The averages were based on the writings of Charles Dow, the founder (along with Edward C. Jones) of *The Wall Street Journal*. The paper originally began publication on July 3, 1982, as the *Customer's Afternoon Letter*, and was renamed on July 8, 1889, with Dow as its first editor. The original Dow Jones Average of 12 stocks* appeared for the first time in the first edition.[†]

After Dow's death, his successor as editor, Samuel Nelson, published a book, *The ABCs of Stock Speculation*, in which the well-known Dow Theory was introduced. The theory is a market-wide version of support and resistance levels. This form of technical analysis is widely followed, even by those who consider themselves faithful only to fundamental analysis. The theory is based on overall movement patterns of stocks, without any regard for economic factors. The Dow Theory is not a gimmick. It is based on the belief that primary movements in the indexes establish very real trends. That does not change the fact that the DJIA is a technical indicator.

In 1916 the list was increased to 20 companies, and on October 1, 1928, it was expanded again to today's level of 30 industrial companies' stocks.[‡]

---

* The original 12 stocks were: American Cotton Oil; American Sugar; American Tobacco; Chicago Gas; Distilling & Cattle Feeding; General Electric; Leclede Gas; National Lead; North American; Tennessee Coal & Iron; U.S. Leather preferred; and U.S. Rubber. Of these, only General Electric remains on the averages today.

[†] For more information and statistics about the DJIA, check the Web site averages.dowjones.com.

[‡] As of the beginning of 1998, the 30 stocks included in the DJIA are: AT&T; AlliedSignal; Aluminum Company of America; American Express; Boeing; Caterpillar; Chevron; Coca-Cola; DuPont; Eastman Kodak; Exxon; General Electric; General Motors; Goodyear Tire & Rubber; Hewlett-Packard; IBM; International Paper; Johnson & Johnson; J.P. Morgan; McDonald's; Merck; 3M; Philip Morris; Proctor & Gamble; Sears; Travelers Group; Union Carbide; United Technologies; Wal-Mart; and Walt Disney.

The theories on which market trend analysis was originally based may be out of date today, in many respects. The world has changed. Transportation and utility companies may not have the kind of market influence in the twenty-first century that they held when Dow first published his ideas. Today there may be greater influence from technology, automation, communications, and other industries.

The "industrial" averages originally were largely financial. Today, the stocks in that average include a more diverse selection of companies, which is appropriate as the world changes and especially as the United States' economy moves away from a manufacturing emphasis and "industry" has become dominant overseas.

The DJIA is the most widely used indicator, believed to show a "central tendency" or trend in the companies represented within the index. But there are several problems with this approach. First, the criteria on which a stock is selected to be included in the DJIA are not published. Second, the index is not weighted to equalize share prices for different companies. As a consequence, companies with higher-priced stock have a correspondingly greater influence on the averages. So when you hear that the market "went up" today, that should not be taken as a broad indicator of market health. It is a summary of what happened in only 30 companies; and those among the 30 with higher capitalization exert greater influence on the level of the index.

From time to time, some stocks are removed from the DJIA, to be replaced with other stocks. Why? What changes led to the removal of one or more companies, and to their replacement with others? How were these more representative, more suitable, or more desirable from the point of view of the market? It is possible that much of the rise in the stock market during so-called bull market periods may be attributed to the selection criteria by Dow Jones & Company, rather than from any specific economic or market-based changes or trends.

A more accurate measure of the market in terms of price movement may be the Dow Jones Composite Index. It covers all stocks included in the industrial, transportation, and utility averages and reports them together. This index, while broader and thus more representative of market movement, has two primary problems. First, it has not caught the imagination of market watchers like the industrial averages have. Second, it represents only 65 stocks, a small portion of the whole market.

The problem with any index that includes only a handful of the thousands of listed companies is that someone has to decide which companies to include. Over the years, the stocks included in the three Dow Jones market indexes have changed. In theory, these changes reflect real changes in the corporate world. But how can we be certain that the makeup of highly selective indexes truly reflect market conditions?

We should be using the broadest possible indexes, if, in fact, we even think that overall market trends are important. The study of indexes may be useful in terms of actual timing of decisions to buy, hold, or sell, but a long-term investment strategy should not depend on today's market trend.

For the purpose of studying broader market trends, a study of the overall market makes more sense, even though it may be less interesting to the financial press. Standard and Poor's (S&P) 500 Composite Index includes 500 companies, compared to the Dow Jones Composite Index's 65. Though the S&P 500 still represents only a portion of the market, it is an improvement over the DJIA for three reasons. First, the S&P 500 is weighted, whereas the DJIA is not. That means that the relative value per share is identical for every company listed, regardless of the value of stock or dollar value of capitalization.

Second, 500 stocks represent a broader picture of "the market," and more accurately. The 500 stocks include 400 industrial companies, 40 utilities, 40 financial companies, and 20 transportation stocks.

Third, the S&P 500 is a true index rather than an average. The starting point, which is the market value of companies from 1941 to 1943, is averaged and then assigned a base value. So a change from the base value is a reflection of market changes, unlike the DJIA, which reports on the current average of stock prices with no equal base.

An even broader representation of the market is found in the New York Stock Exchange (NYSE) Composite Index. This is an average of prices for all stocks listed on the NYSE. The National Association of Securities Dealers Automated Quotations (Nasdaq) indexes, which began tracking on February 5, 1971, reflect price movement of the thousands of stocks traded not on the NYSE, but on the over the counter (OTC) market. The value of stocks is weighted so that, like the S&P 500, the Nasdaq indexes more fairly represent market trends than the DJIA. These far broader measurements include only United States–listed securities. Many trends in our domestic market are reflections of events overseas. So even a broader U.S. index may not truly reflect short-term trends in this country.

These methods of measuring the current mood of the market have become the obsession of Wall Street. Most of the analysis work found in financial publications arises from opinion and application of technical analysis based on a study of averages—in other words, short-term trends. These have no effect on long-term financial profit or loss.

Another interesting observation concerning index obsession is this: The more rational the index, the less interesting it is to the market watchers. This is a consistent pattern. The famous DJIA includes only 30 companies and yet, to many, it is the market. The more representative composite indexes, which attempt to capture all company stock trends, are largely ignored and often go unreported.

With computerization, you might expect fundamental information to improve in quality and availability. This is true. However, the primary change with automation has been an expansion of technical analysis. Today, the study of indexes has expanded and become highly specialized. Industry groups are studied regularly, not to mention foreign market trends, and technical trends in commodities, options, bonds, and other nonstock investments.

The computer has served to make the technician more efficient at producing opinion; it has not necessarily improved on the quality of that opinion. Graphic capability has made it easy to produce charts quickly and for a wide and diverse number of stocks, industry groups, and indexes. This never improves the quality of information; it only makes quantifying easier. So even with more reliable scaling, faster output, and greatly improved turnaround time, questionable information remains questionable.

How the Numbers Help

Moving beyond the observations of technical analysis and its shortcomings, the next question should be: How do the numbers help in making investment decisions? In other words, what can you gain as an investor by studying last year's financial statement?

Every investor faces the same problem: trying to develop reliable information based on hindsight as a means for making decisions requiring foresight. Poorly made decisions often are a matter of timing, which points out the flaw of short-term investing. The market rewards shareholders through long-term increases in value; that is to say, profits. Short-term investing, also called speculation, involves the potential for statistically higher profits, but also for much greater risks. Thus, buying newly issued stock in a start-up corporation could result in fantastic profits or in a complete loss. Buying a dependable 100 shares in a blue chip company that has been around for 150 years involves far less risk and far less excitement.

The decision to buy stock today, to hold it tomorrow, or to sell it in 10 or 15 years, has to be based on some sensible plan. Long-term investors usually have a specific goal in mind; for example, college education for a child or retirement. They rely on a specific outcome in terms of profit for a goal to be met. You cannot afford your child's college education if you lose your entire investment, and you cannot afford retirement if the value of your capital has been eroded by inflation, taxes, and a series of badly timed decisions. In comparison, investors who speculate and think short-term may be more addicted to the excitement in the deal—buying and selling—and less committed to reaching a goal in 10 or 20 years. All of us have to decide which category defines our attitude toward the market.

With all of these potential risks in mind, we come back to the big question: How do the numbers help? Remember, it is not only the decision to buy or not to buy a particular stock that is so critical, but the ongoing decision to continue holding and, ultimately, the decision about selling. All of these decisions will be good or bad depending both on fundamental tests and on timing. The numbers themselves help you to identify the wisdom of a decision at a particular time. Some examples illustrate this point.

Example: You are thinking about buying stock in a particular company that has a long history of profits, consistent payment of dividends, and clear dominance in its industry. In the past two years, though, the stock has fallen slightly, contrary to its history of steadily growing value. A study of fundamentals shows several things. First, one-time adjustments were made for foreign exchange losses. Second, profits were lower than forecast due to a change in the method of valuation of inventory. Third, the corporation recently acquired several other companies, whose losses are reflected in the consolidated financial statements. You believe that the recent poor performance in the stock is temporary. Your fundamental analysis tells you that the unpopularity of this stock is short-term, temporary, and ill-founded. This is an excellent time to invest in this company.

In this example, you could identify the probable causes of poor market performance, where perception is more important than reality. The stock may be undervalued. A technical interpretation of the same company, based only on stock movement, might be entirely different and perhaps misleading, because it would not be based on an analysis of financial fact. This is a good example of how the numbers help you to make a decision. By identifying why the stock's market value has fallen, and realizing that the influences were temporary and not likely to affect long-term value, you saw a buying opportunity.

Example: You bought 300 shares in a company's stock two years ago and you have been monitoring the company's financial statements. The stock yielded between 5 percent and 7 percent each year and its market value rose modestly. However, in comparing this company's stock to that of its industry competitors, you realize that dominance in the industry is changing. On the basis of gross sales, the company you chose used to hold a clear lead. Today, though, a competitor has taken over that position. An analysis of financial trends for both corporations has convinced you that the competitor has greater potential for future profit. You decide to sell your stock and invest in the other company.

➹ KEY POINT

Long-term investing does not require that you stop studying financial trends. Ongoing analysis is of critical importance. The "hold" decision is subject to change when fundamental analysis indicates the need.

This example shows that at times, a long-term strategy and a "hold" decision must be changed. By comparing the stock currently held to that of a close competitor, you will gain insight in terms of changing trends and relative value. Many investors study only the fundamentals of the company selected, ignoring the equally important trends of competitors and of industry-wide changes.

As you begin studying the fundamentals with long-term concerns in mind, you gain a broader market perspective. The energy that many people put into watching today's trends—rumor, chart movements, and so forth—could be better used in studying the market from afar, ignoring the day-to-day tendencies of the market, and in general, avoiding the attractive but useless excitement associated with momentary change. To some degree, the hype associated with short-term trends is similar to what some journalists do. They fill the papers and television with the sensational, short-term, and the meaningless to keep us interested and to compete with one another. In the market, the possibility of a crash, an opportunity to get rich overnight, and the potential for getting the edge on everyone else are difficult to ignore, and they make great copy. However, if you look back at the daily financial news from a month ago, a year ago, or a decade ago, you begin to see how empty and useless it really is to what you need and want—guidance and a plan for managing your investment capital now and in the future.

Why You Cannot Afford to Ignore the Numbers

The point has been made that today's technical trends, including the DJIA, are of little or no value to your long-term investment success. However, while the daily news is of no significance in the bigger picture, you still must watch financial trends on a regular basis. This may not be necessary from day to day, but it does not hurt to keep abreast of emerging trends and tendencies that affect your investments.

When you compare the different forms of analysis available—remembering that *all* analysis is intended to forecast the future—fundamental analysis becomes the obvious choice for determining likely outcomes. Certainly, businesses depend on fundamentals. Stock market investors may learn much from the value of the business exercise of financial analysis. Accountants and other managers spend much of their time analyzing past results in an attempt to make forecasts. The exercise of forecasting sales, costs, and expenses is recognized as one of the most valuable routines undertaken in the corporate world. For the purpose of identifying future market opportunities, consumer preferences, competitive trends, and the cost of doing business, the corporate culture is rooted deeply in the idea that forecasting the future is a valuable, important, and necessary part of management.

✦ *KEY POINT*

If forecasting is of such obvious importance in corporations, where profits are all-important, investors may expect to succeed by applying the same principles to their own portfolios.

Making Fundamental Information Available

Fundamental information is not difficult to find. For listed corporations, it is widely published. Market research services are affordable and readily available, and the financial press is up to date and reliable. The Internet, too, contains a vast array of information. Perhaps the biggest problem with these sources is deciding what to use from among all of the market information you can find easily.

The next chapter talks about some of the problems with the fundamentals, and how timing is critical to the market decision-making process. You need to depend on information that may be weeks or even months old by the time it is published. The critical information you learn, though, is not what is taking place right this minute, but as part of the trend for that particular company. Keep the following two areas of distinction in mind when you look for financial information.

1. Long-Term Thinking Is Different from Short-Term Thinking

Today's news is not valuable as long-term information. It is only the latest element in a series of data that, when added together, paint a complete picture of a trend. The immediate news, even when it is purely intrinsic in nature, cannot be viewed in isolation or used to make an investment decision. How that latest piece of information fits with the total picture is what counts. To see the total picture, you need comparative analysis among companies in the same industry, among companies whose stock you are thinking of buying (or selling), and between one company's current and past results.

2. The Stock Price Is Not the Same as Financial Results

Great emphasis is put on the current market value of stock, in the belief that it is a reflection of financial results. That is not true. The stock price reflects current perceptions of value, which may have little or nothing to do with the company's financial status. In fact, market value per share (the current price of stock) often is vastly different than the company's real intrinsic capital value, also known as book value per share. These two values—stock price and book value—have nothing to do with one another. Stock price represents the price agreed on by buyers and sellers at a particular moment. It is the highest price a buyer is willing to pay for stock and the lowest price a seller is willing to accept. When more buyers are available, the price is driven upward; when more sellers are available, the price is driven downward. Market price results purely from the forces of supply and demand.

In comparison, book value per share is the intrinsic value of a share of stock. To compute this value, first find the capital value of the company; that is, the total net worth minus any intangible assets. (Intangible assets include items like goodwill, which has no dollar value but which affects a company's stability, strength, and investment value.) Divide the net worth by the number of outstanding shares of common stock. This calculation is summarized in Figure 1.2.

FIGURE 1.2   Book Value Per Share

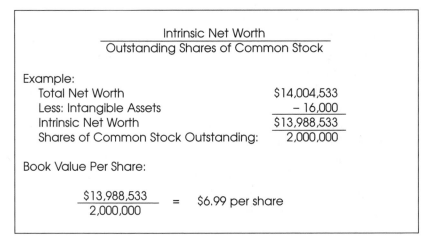

$$\frac{\text{Intrinsic Net Worth}}{\text{Outstanding Shares of Common Stock}}$$

Example:

Total Net Worth	$14,004,533
Less: Intangible Assets	– 16,000
Intrinsic Net Worth	$13,988,533
Shares of Common Stock Outstanding:	2,000,000

Book Value Per Share:

$$\frac{\$13,988,533}{2,000,000} = \$6.99 \text{ per share}$$

In the example, book value per share is about $7. In comparing this to the market price of a share of stock, you are likely to find no relationship between the two values. For many reasons discussed earlier, market price could be substantially higher or lower than book value per share.

Make It Simple

Any program devised to help you make more informed decisions will work only if it is practical and easy to use. While this may seem obvious, remember that it is easy to fall into the trap of overcomplicating the task of developing a program for analysis. Keep these points in mind:

- *Keep it simple.* Study the numbers, know what you are looking for, and act on the information you develop.
- *Comparison is the key.* A particular company should be reviewed in terms of how its direct competitors look, and how their fundamentals size up. A particular industry also should be compared to others, so that your range of possible investment alternatives is not limited to one sector alone.
- *Learn all you can about fundamental techniques.* While simplicity is the key, meaning that you must limit the scope of your self-designed program, you will also need to consider an array of fundamental techniques that you might want to employ.
- *Reexamine your portfolio regularly.* Investment decisions are never final. The decision you make today might be viewed differently in light of future information. When you discover that the fundamentals have changed, an ongoing "hold" decision might be incorrect. Likewise, your rejection of one company today might be subject to change in a year or two.
- *The decision to take no action is also a decision.* Investors might overlook the importance of the "hold" decision. Inaction is as important as buying or selling.
- *Don't discount technical analysis completely.* You probably cannot avoid exposure to the DJIA or the financial news in general, where technical analysis rules and today's rumors have much weight. However, technical indicators create undervalued and overvalued stocks, information that can be valuable to you.
- *Never stop researching.* You need an efficient, working program that you like and understand, and to establish a schedule and routine to monitor the market according to your own program.

CHAPTER 2

Timing of Financial Information— Yesterday's News

*I*n any reading of financial statements, keep in mind the fact that the information is dated. Even a report produced immediately after the close of the period in question is out of date because a new period has begun. It is not reliable to base today's status on yesterday's report.

History, however, is useful and may be instructive about the future. We can make some reasonable calculations about the present and the future, based on a corporation's financial statements from last month or last year.

The Problem of Financial Information

Those companies with publicly traded stock are regulated by the Securities and Exchange Commission (SEC), the federal oversight agency created as part of the Securities Act of 1933. The SEC has authority to regulate the securities business and especially the reporting of financial information by publicly traded companies. This includes information reported in a prospectus, a registration statement, and financial statements. It also includes the power to prescribe the form for submitting information, accounting and auditing methods, and procedures used in valuation and calculations. In other words, the SEC has broad powers to impose and enforce requirements on companies reporting financial results to you, the shareholder—even to the extent that the company's value and financial results are affected. SEC regulations are not merely advisory. The SEC can institute civil proceedings against companies not following its regulations and, in cases of extreme noncompliance or reporting fraud, it may file criminal charges. Penalties could include fines and even imprisonment for offenders.

In addition to having to comply with SEC regulations and submit to SEC audits, publicly listed companies are required to undergo periodic audits by independent certified public accounting firms. Accounting and auditing standards include more than 2,000 pages of rulings, procedures, and pronouncements issued by the accounting industry's national association, the American Institute of Certified Public Accountants (AICPA). The AICPA oversight of its own members has evolved into voluntary cooperation with another national board, the Financial Accounting Standards Board (FASB). This board has no authority or power of its own, but serves as a coordinating agency for the AICPA as well as numerous other agencies, including the SEC. The FASB actually sets accounting standards and makes rules in cooperation with the industry as a whole and with agreement from several involved agencies.

What has grown out of this large regulatory environment is a single national standard. This is a safeguard for investors. The rules, overall, are referred to as generally accepted accounting principles (GAAP). A GAAP rule mandates the methods to be used for reporting financial transactions.

To the nonaccountant, it might be puzzling that such a wide array of standards and procedures are necessary. After all, a transaction occurs and should be reported accurately. Where is the debate? In fact, though, a large number of decisions must be made that can affect value and profits significantly. There is a need for consistent treatment of many financial transactions. Some of these are:

- The valuation of inventory
- Placing a value on foreign exchange profit or loss
- Placing a dollar value on a reserve for bad debts
- Depreciation methods
- Treatment of extraordinary loss, unusual expenses, and nonrecurring expenses
- Simple timing

The auditor's job is to apply GAAP as consistently as possible. At times, the company's accounting department will disagree with an auditor's interpretation of the rules, and a discussion has to be held to settle the issue. With more than 2,000 pages of guidelines, it is entirely possible that each side may find some rule supporting its position. At times, the auditor is placed in the position of compromising with the company's accountant, and modifying its proposed adjustments. This does not mean the financial statement is not prepared honestly. As a rule, accountants and auditors want to report honestly the financial data for the company. Accountants and auditors have to determine which treatment best reflects the actual results for the year. The consequences of the treatment decision can be significant for the company's profit and, ultimately, for its stock's market price as well.

🗝 KEY POINT

The purpose of creating accounting standards is to strive for consistent and honest reporting. Still, much interpretation may occur, making comparisons difficult from one period to another, and from one company to another.

It takes several weeks of auditing and analysis just to ensure that the auditors agree with what the company has reported. Invariably, some adjustments are made as part of the audit. So the company cannot issue a financial statement with any confidence until the audit has been completed.

Timing of Financial News

The stock market moves quickly. Stock prices change not only from day to day, but from minute to minute. When one particular stock attracts a lot of interest, the changes in price can be quite dramatic and exciting to watch. Timing is everything.

This is a problem for those who believe in fundamental analysis. There is no instant fundamental information available, and financial statements are normally two or three months old by the time they are read. This situation should be thought of in light of an earlier observation: The moment-to-moment changes in the market, movements in the indexes, and news or gossip have no long-term effect on the investment decisions you make today. Technical indicators and the immediate news affect the overall market in the moment, but fundamental analysis has great value for long-term investment decisions—and absolutely no excitement right now.

๑ KEY POINT

Fundamental analysis is not very exciting, but it is dependable as a means for judging a company's growth potential. It is easy to be distracted by gossip and rumor, but ultimately, long-term investing depends on a study of the fundamentals.

Published financial statements cannot be used for day-to-day decisions. Because the information is outdated, financial statements offer absolutely nothing of value to the speculator. The historical record might be of interest, but in truth, the speculator is far more interested in technical indicators: the movement of stock price, high and low levels compared to today's market value, the stock's most recent chart, its tendency to react (or overreact) to the market as a whole, and other such measures. These indicators are available every day and, with automation, even on an instantly updated basis. Thus, they appear to offer more insight and information to the investor. The speculator cannot afford to care about financial strength or stability, profits, quality of management, competitive position of the company, or other fundamental tests. Only one thing matters: the market price now and its potential for dramatic change in the immediate future.

The trap in using only technical indicators is that they are tied to indexes or visual trading patterns (charts and graphs), or they attempt to assess market value based on formulas tied to past price movement. In other words, if you really believe in the fundamentals, then such technical indicators are not reliable—they are only easily available.

๑ KEY POINT

Mere availability of information does not make that information useful. Investors need to seek reliability rather than convenience.

It is a serious error to opt for market intelligence merely because it is easily available and up-to-date. Some technical indicators can provide value to you as a part of your overall selection and decision-making process, but using it alone makes no sense for selection of long-term investments.

Historical versus Current Information

One way to distinguish between fundamental and technical analysis is on the basis of point of view. Fundamentals are historical; technical indicators are current or forward-looking. Of course, the technical indicators are not based on any reliable historical information, so the entire premise of operating from the current date forward, is flawed—if it takes place in isolation.

The Dow Jones Industrial Average makes the point well. If the average moves more than 100 points in either direction, that causes a reaction among large numbers of investors. Some see the direction of the move as a sign of a shift in market sentiment; others believe the shift will be reversed the following day. Many investors track historical movement of the market and what they believe it means for the future. For example, some believe that if the index goes up in January it will go up for the entire year, and vice versa. Others believe that market movements are dictated by whether the National League or American League team wins the World Series.

All of these attempts at forecasting are flawed and cannot provide any long-term wisdom. You cannot predict "heads" or "tails" for a coin toss based on the trend, because each toss is a separate and random trial with a 50–50 possibility. Most of us know that. But when it comes to the market, the desire for reliable and easily identified indicators is strong. Ultimately, even the technician comes to grips with the problems of forecasting and returns to the fundamentals. The flaw in many technical indicators is that historical information is misread or misapplied. The same thinking about trying to predict coin tosses should be kept in mind. A chart reader, for example, will see a pattern of a stock's market price moving up, then down, then up, and will reason that based on that pattern, the next movement will be downward. This is not supported with any economic theory whatsoever. Three things can happen to the market price of a stock: it can rise, it can fall, or it can remain unchanged. So even the wildest of theories will turn out right at least one-third of the time.

✿ KEY POINT

The flaw in technical analysis is that it can deceive you. Price movements do not occur strictly because of a pattern developed in the past. Price movement reflects ever-changing perceptions of value and current supply and demand.

Where does technical historical information help? Some of the information we learn from technical indicators is useful, but primarily because it is actually a hybrid of technical and fundamental information. For our purposes here, we've named this hybrid "technimental." We define technimental analysis as any form of analysis based on technical indicators, but containing elements of fundamental analysis; or that provides useful information of a fundamental nature.

The most obvious example of technimental analysis is the trading range seen in the technician's chart (see Figure 1.1), notably a long-established range with a clear resistance level (the highest expected price the stock has traded) and support level (the lowest expected trading price in the range). The trading range provides us with a fundamental view of the stock's supply and demand. Remembering that the stock price itself has nothing to do with book value per share, nor with long-term prospects for the stock, what can you hope to learn from an analysis of the trading range? As a long-term investor, you do need to keep an eye on your portfolio and long-term decisions have to be maintained (or changed) based on a study of short-term trends. While this refers primarily to the information on the company's balance sheet and statement of income, the trading range can be useful in identifying one of two important changes: (1) buying opportunities or (2) selling signals.

The trading range is a reflection of the market's perception about the stock. As a broad observation, such perceptions are based on long-term understanding of the fundamentals, and daily changes are not especially useful. That's where resistance and support levels can provide a signal of possible change, especially when the trading range has been long established or has been changing only gradually. A breakout may be temporary, or it may mean a significant change in the market's entire perception about that company, thereby raising the resistance level or lowering the support level.

Example: You have been watching one company's stock for several months, studying the fundamentals and thinking about investing. You also have observed the gradual climb in the stock's market value over time. At the same time you have observed a gradual change in several financial trends, indicating the possibility that the company is taking a leading position within its industry. A breakout above resistance level could serve as the final indicator inducing you to take action and buy the stock.

In this example, a breakout following a long-standing trading range serves as a technimental indicator. Because fundamentals work long-term, you should be cautious in using technical indicators for such decisions. In the example, the breakout served to confirm a trend already being observed. This is the only situation in which technical indicators should be relied on—when they confirm what seems to be occurring and is already indicated in the fundamental trend.

🏃 KEY POINT

A technical indicator should be relied on for making a decision only when it confirms the trend already seen in the fundamental analysis.

Another example demonstrates how such information can be used to make a "sell" decision:

Example: You have held 200 shares of a company's stock for four years. Recent fundamental trends seem to indicate that the company is beginning to lose its position as industry leader. However, you are reluctant to sell until you are certain that the indications are correct. You also have been tracking the chart of the stock's movement and you notice a gradual decline in the trading range, but dependable support levels over many months. However, the stock then fell through the support level and declined to a new low. It recently recovered, but it is apparent to you now that perceptions of this company's value have fallen. You decide to sell.

This is yet another example of basing a decision on both the generally indicated trend in the fundamental tests, and confirmation from a long-standing technical indicator. This shows how technimental information can be used in combination with fundamental tests for managing your portfolio.

The market price of the stock is far removed from the fundamental value of the company. The justification for using technical indicators is to confirm trends recognized by fundamental tests. Even the most ardent fundamental analyst needs to recognize the reality of the market: Stock price is the reflection of the market's perception of value. The price is the result of auction activity between buyers and sellers. So even when the price is entirely unreasonable based on the fundamental facts of the matter, the market price cannot be ignored.

Stock Price as the Basic Indicator

Most investors will agree that the stock's current market price per share is a basic indicator. For most of us, price is the first impression we have of a stock. The stock market is an auction marketplace because buyers and sellers cause stock prices to move based on their own perceptions of value and the price they are willing to pay. A greater number of buyers, all bidding on a relatively limited number of shares for sale, drive up the per-share price. A greater number of sellers, all seeking a relatively limited number of willing buyers, drive down the per-share price.

> ### ✦ KEY POINT
>
> Supply and demand for shares of stock is what sets that stock's price. While fundamentals have a long-term effect, day-to-day price movements reflect only the immediate perception of value.

Market price works as a basic indicator even for the fundamental analyst. We know that market price is an immediate measurement of the market's perception of value. It may have nothing to do with fundamentals, at least directly. However, if a particular company's stock is chronically below the level where it should be, there usually is a reason. That reason may be found in the fundamentals.

Example: In one industry, stock prices generally fall within a specified range in comparison to earnings, (also called the PE ratio, or price-earnings ratio—more on this later in the chapter). One stock, however, trades at a very low PE when compared to others. You wonder why.

It is wise to wonder why a PE ratio for one company would be exceptionally low (or exceptionally high) compared to the industry average. As an investor, you expect an investment candidate to fit the model as dictated by tests that you depend on for information. You may be sure that the answer to exceptionally low PE ratios will be found in the fundamentals, because the market perception about a company's value does not occur in a vacuum. This is why the price and the PE ratio are important tests. Some investors believe that it is possible to find exceptional values that everyone else has missed. In fact, some short-term only buying opportunities can be found. The market tends to adjust pricing of stocks based on the fundamentals, the most important of which is earnings. This is why the PE ratio is one of the most popular and important tests used by investors. It shows how the market views a particular stock based on earnings.

⚡ KEY POINT

You are wise to question why a particular stock's PE ratio is exceptionally low or exceptionally high. Invariably there is a reason, and that reason is important information for you as an investor.

Stock price also should be compared to book value per share. While this is not commonly used as an indicator for purposes of forecasting future value like the PE ratio does, book value per share remains an important fundamental test. If market value per share is vastly higher than book value, you might wonder why the market has such high esteem for the stock. There may be good reason, or it may indicate a corresponding exaggeration in the PE ratio. Wide disparity between stock price and book value per share can be a danger signal. Likewise, what does it mean if market price is very close to book value per share, or even lower? This indicates very little market interest in future prospects for that stock. It could mean there exists a real opportunity; it is more likely that market perception is dependable and should not be ignored.

Why is the difference between market price of stock and book value per share so interesting? Investors do not pay much attention to book value per share. Chances are good that most investors would not be able to even tell you the book value of their stock if asked, whereas many would know the PE ratio. But the comparison is important—because even though the fundamentals are the key to smart long-term investing, accounting is an imperfect art. The methods used for reporting a company's worth and profits are far from perfect.

🏃 KEY POINT

Market perception reflects future potential, which may be more reliable than the more rigid conventions of financial reporting.

Accounting rules are conservative. For example, a company might own vast land holdings for many years, but the true market value of that land must be reported in the books at original cost. So you cannot tell from studying the balance sheet what a company's real net worth per share would be if the company were to be liquidated. Book value per share reflects the conservative reporting required under accounting rules. It does not reflect what the market perceives or knows about that company's growth prospects, the real value of its assets, or its potential to out-compete other companies in its industry.

In the 1970s and 1980s when takeovers defined large segments of the market, these problems became glaringly obvious. Some companies were taken over primarily because someone recognized that the real value of the company's assets was greater than the market value and certainly greater than book value per share. It was possible to acquire a controlling interest in a corporation and sell off its parts—land, subsidiaries, inventory—and make a profit greater than the acquisition cost.

Useful Current Indicators

Among the range of fundamental indicators, three are particularly useful for quick comparison and analysis: (1) total sales, (2) net margin, and (3) PE ratio.

All indicators have to be reviewed in comparative form, or they have no value. As you study fundamental information, keep in mind the various methods of comparison that add meaning and value to the numbers. These include:

- *Within one industry.* Stock selection often involves comparing stock of each of the corporations within a targeted industry. The dominant role within the industry is important as a growth indicator because the leading company has the best prospects for future growth.
- *Year to year.* Financial information, especially income-related results, has value and reveals information primarily when compared to past periods. Even a two-year comparison is limited in value, whereas a five-year or ten-year comparison shows a clear trend.
- *Between different industries.* Look at two or more industries to gauge relative strength. Apply the basic tests between industries to judge the relative growth potential of a particular company or group of companies.
- *Within a predetermined range.* Some fundamental indicators are better when held to a consistent standard and not constantly growing. We expect the dollar amount of sales to rise over time as an indication of continuing growth. However, the percentage of sales going to profits (net margin) should remain constant. It cannot be expected to rise each year. A recurring, dependable rate of return should be expected in a well-managed company. So comparisons between companies or industries may be made not for a rising trend line, but in search of a flat one, a consistent rate of return.

Sales

Sales are the most common and best understood indicator for any business. If sales are rising, the company is growing. In fact, rising sales are the most consistent method for defining growth, and a company with growth prospects needs expanding markets and market share. You can easily find sales figures for the current year and past years by studying research reports or by contacting the company through the mail, on the Internet, or with the assistance of a brokerage firm. Meaningful analysis requires not only a tracking of the sales volume, but identification of the underlying causes for that volume. Did sales occur as the result of higher unit sales or raised prices? Or do improved numbers reflect the results of acquisitions? Are falling sales in line with industry rates? Either answer largely determines the significance of changes in sales volume.

Sales results are widely available and should be tracked carefully. The trend is of great importance, because many companies peak out at some point. The peak is quickly recognized by its pattern, such as the one shown in Figure 2.1.

FIGURE 2.1 Sales Plateau Pattern

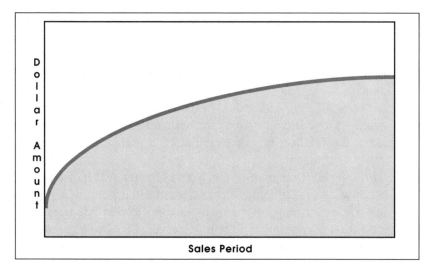

Note that the trend, while rising in the past, flattens out and stops rising. There is no way to predict when (or if) this will happen in a particular company, but it does occur. Growth has natural limitations, even in large, well-financed, and well-managed companies. This is first reflected in the plateau effect and is seen in sales.

The company's sales results are reported regularly, often in advance of the publication of a final financial statement. Sales are fairly easy to track and report and not subject to adjustment in the same degree as other financial results so companies often announce their sales levels fairly soon after the close of each quarter.

Net Margin

The second readily available indicator is the net margin, the comparison between sales and profits. Compute by dividing net profit by total sales; the result is expressed as a percentage. This formula is summarized in Figure 2.2.

FIGURE 2.2 Net Margin

$$\frac{\text{Net Profit}}{\text{Total Shares}}$$

Example:
  Total Sales $42,854,063
  Net Profit $3,366,983
  Net Margin   7.86%

$$\frac{\$42,854,063}{\$3,366,983} \quad = \quad 7.86\%$$

With any formula, you need to ensure that you use the correct figure. Otherwise, comparisons will not be valid. In the case of net profit, you may run into problems because three different versions of net profit may be found on the financial statement.

The first is operating profit, which is simply the result of subtracting the "cost of sales," and "selling, general, and administrative expenses" from total sales. The result is the profit produced from selling the company's products or services. It does not include income or expenses not directly related to the sale of the product or service, and also excludes income taxes.

Second is the net profit before taxes, which includes all forms of income and expense, whether or not directly related to the production of sales. These may include income or loss from foreign exchange, interest income and expense, and other nonoperational adjustments.

Third is the net profit (or net profit after taxes), meaning the profit after including all income and deducting all costs and expenses. This is the final number that should be used for calculation of net margin. It is consistent, and it allows for all items, including those items not directly related to operations of the corporation.

Net margin is one of those comparative features of financial analysis that should be steady and consistent. The more consistent, the better. A dependable, consistent net margin, year after year, is a sign of a well-managed corporation. If management is able to maintain that level even when sales are growing over time, it is a positive indicator. Too often, analysts and investors come to expect all factors to improve from year to year. Just as sales are expected to rise, so are net profits and the net margin. This is not realistic. You cannot expect net profits to grow at a greater rate than other financial factors. There is such an unavoidable relationship between sales and costs that net profits will not exceed the yield range on a consistent basis. To expect that to occur ignores the realities and economics of corporate and competitive life.

🔑 KEY POINT

Don't fall into the trap of expecting yields to rise every year. A more valuable sign is the ability of a corporation's management to produce acceptable yield levels consistently year after year.

PE Ratio

The final feature to look for on a regular basis is the price-earnings, or PE ratio. This popular measure is published in the financial listings in most instances, and is considered a dependable means for making comparisons among a broad range of stocks.

As a means for judging value, the PE ratio is the most widely followed. It is not strictly a fundamental indicator, however. It combines one critically important piece of financial information (earnings per share) with the current market price of the stock. You will recall that market value reflects the current perception of value, and may have no direct bearing on the book value per share or the real future prospects for growth. So PE ratio is partially a reflection of current popularity. An accountant will argue that book value per share is the only valid test of a company's value, but accountants do not think in the same way as investors think, especially in a market where prices are subject to minute-by-minute auction.

PE value is calculated by dividing the stock's current price per share by the annual earnings per share of common stock. The value of earnings per share is an important fundamental indicator on its own. It is the calculated value of earnings for the latest reported period—usually the latest quarter—divided by the number of outstanding shares of common stock. The formula for earnings per share is shown in Figure 2.3.

(Be sure that when comparing PE ratios between companies, the earning period being reported is consistent. You will distort the comparison if one company uses the most recent fiscal quarter, whereas another is based on a previous 12-month fiscal year.)

FIGURE 2.3 Earnings Per Share

$$\frac{\text{Annual Earnings}}{\text{Outstanding Shares of Common Stock}}$$

Example:
   Annual Earnings $42,941,100
   Outstanding Shares of Common Stock   11,450,960

$$\frac{\$42,941,100}{11,450,960} \ = \ \$3.75$$

In considering the validity of PE ratio, remember that you are comparing current information (market value of stock) to past information that becomes increasingly outdated with time (last year's earnings per share). The formula for PE ratio is summarized in Figure 2.4.

FIGURE 2.4 PE Ratio

$$\frac{\text{Price Per Share}}{\text{Annual Earnings Per Share}}$$

Example:
   Price Per Share of Stock $45.00
   Annual Earnings Per Share $3.75
   PE Ratio   12

$$\frac{\$45.00}{\$3.75} \ = \ 12$$

The current price means the ending price of the stock as of the latest trading day. When you read a stock listing in the financial press, the reported PE ratio is a comparison between the day's closing price and the latest annual earnings per share. The PE ratio is imperfect, like most ratios, because it is reporting in a stationary manner a comparison that is constantly moving. The ending market price may reflect a change completely unrelated to the earning power of the corporation. By its nature, the annual earnings per share is already outdated by the time the information has become available. Still, the PE ratio is valuable because it shows in an efficient manner what the market's perception of a stock's value is at a particular moment.

If you think about what the comparison between market price and earnings per share means, you can gain some insight into what the PE ratio provides in the way of information. The ratio tells you what the market believes a dollar of earnings is worth. In other words, you may ask the question: What does the market believe this stock's potential future earnings are, based on what it has earned most recently? The PE ratio answers this question. By comparing the PE ratio of many corporations, you begin to see that some stocks are currently very popular, while others are less popular or not at all popular. When the fundamentals are otherwise identical, the PE ratio reports the current market perception of potential earnings power, or what the market believes will occur in the future.

An extremely low PE ratio indicates a perception that the company is not especially exciting at the moment. Investors believe the future growth potential is not as attractive as the companies for which relatively high PE ratios are being paid today. So as a general rule, high PE ratios indicate that the company's growth prospects are better than average; and low PE ratios indicate the opposite—at least as those matters are perceived today.

There is a flip side to the PE ratio. As that ratio gets higher, it also means that the market as a whole is assigning great value to future earnings potential. In other words, high PE ratios reflect higher demand because the market believes the company will grow at better than average rates. If we remember that the market invariably overreacts to all news—good or bad—it is also possible that some stock prices are inflated because of that overreaction. It often means that a stock's market price is unrealistically high. Hence, higher risks can sometimes be identified by unusually high PE ratios or, more to the point, a rapidly rising PE ratio compared to past ratio levels. The market price can become more volatile when it is inflated in this manner. Even the hint of negative news could cause an overreaction in the opposite direction, invariably meaning the stock's market value will fall.

Example: The stock of one company has reported record earnings in recent years, and it has become popular among investors. The PE ratio was consistently in the 8-to-12 range for several years but during the past year, the stock's price has risen rapidly. The PE ratio rose to 35 in a matter of only a few months. More recently, it went to 60. Last week, a report was published estimating that prior estimates of earnings for the company would not be realized; and forecasts were revised to report that rather than realizing an 11 percent net margin, the company is now expected to net only 9 percent. When this news hit the press, the stock's price fell rapidly.

This type of cause and effect is not unusual. A PE ratio is great as an immediate indicator because it compares perception of value (current market price) to the fundamentals (earnings per share). It is an easy and fast measurement of perception. So when a stock's PE ratio is steady and within an average range (whatever average means for that particular stock), you can use that as a test of the stock's price stability. That means the market perception has not changed dramatically in recent times. But when the PE ratio changes suddenly—often accompanied by sudden changes in market price—that could mean that near-term volatility may be expected. It could also mean that some other change is afoot. Perhaps it means that nothing fundamentally noteworthy has occurred and the market, as a whole, is simply overreacting to earnings or price, or both.

Because earnings vary between companies, you can expect to see a wide range of PE ratios among different stocks. There is no safe or dependable way to equate PE levels to prices or to earnings, because market perceptions are odd. For example, many investors have particular biases toward certain stocks because of their trading price range. They might like stocks selling between $10 and $25 per share, but avoid any stocks selling above that level. This is illogical, because the market price reflects only the current demand versus the number of shares outstanding. If a company has 12 million shares at $60 per share, it can easily split and reissue $24 million shares at $30 per share. We know that there is no difference in the overall value when this occurs, but for a variety of illogical reasons, price perception exists and you need to be aware of it.

PE ratio gives you a glimpse into the psychology of the market; and that is where it is truly valuable. By comparing the PE ratios of many stocks, you gain a sense of risk and volatility. You come to the point of being able to identify real potential growth based on the fundamentals and influenced by market price changes, by watching PE ratio trends. You should certainly pick stocks with risk in mind, remembering that risk comes in many forms. PE ratio reflects current market risk, also meaning market price risk. Higher PE ratio stocks contain more risk, while also offering higher potential growth. This means greater volatility in stock market price. This observation has been confirmed by studies. One extensive study included a broad-ranging analysis of market risk in five classifications, from highest PE ratios down to the lowest. This study concluded that lower PE ratio stocks produced higher returns than high PE ratio stocks by about 7 percent per year.[*]

✦ KEY POINT

The PE ratio is one way to compare relative risk. High PE ratio stocks offer greater growth potential and more risk; low PE ratio stocks offer less growth potential and less risk.

PE ratios for the overall market tend to increase when the market is rising, as measured by the indexes previously discussed, and to fall as sentiments turn more pessimistic. So the PE ratios also offer a way to measure overall market thinking in broader terms, as well as tests for individual stocks. Be aware that PE ratios typically vary from one industry to another. It is wise to analyze PE ratio trends for industry groups before drawing any comparisons for stocks in different industries. You may study a series of stocks, compare industries, or isolate a single industry and use the PE ratio to judge relative popularity of one company over another. The important point to remember about PE ratios is the relationship between growth potential and risk. Use the PE ratio to develop your own method for analysis.

---

[*] Sanjoy Basu study of 1977; 14-month study of approximately 500 NYSE issues. The Basu study confirmed earlier findings by David Dremen, who tracked 1,200 stocks from 1968 through 1977, showing that holding stocks over nine years produces 7.89 percent average annual return (lowest PE ratio stocks) versus only .33 percent (highest PE ratio stocks).

CHAPTER 3

The Reliability Problem— Accuracy of the Numbers

*F*inancial reports, while generally reliable and accurate, do not always reflect what is really happening in a company. If fundamental analysts make decisions based on a financial statement that is not entirely true and correct, then the fundamental analysis will be misleading.

The procedural rules imposed on the accounting and auditing professions by the Financial Accounting Standards Board, the American Institute of Certified Public Accountants, and the Securities and Exchange Commission (SEC) (as well as state agencies) are intended to set down specific reporting rules. However, in the complexity of the rules themselves, it is possible to find more than one interpretation of how data should be presented. In the financial world, it is possible to substantially affect financial statements and annual reports by tinkering with the numbers. This is disturbing for several reasons. First, if it is possible for a statement to be misrepresented, we next have to wonder if the practice is widespread. Second, if results are commonly misrepresented, then how reliable are the fundamentals?

A KEY POINT

Outright fraud is rare, but the rules allow management broad discretion for interpretation of their own financial results.

Fortunately, significant tinkering—to the point of fraud—is a rare event. Yet, you should be aware that such abuses can and do occur.

The accounting rules are broad enough that companies have considerable latitude, and much of the accounting process involves estimates. What you hope the reporting reflects is a best efforts attempt at reporting the quality of earnings for operations, rather than an artificial reflection of positive results. Some interpretations are conservative, while others are aggressive. As a shareholder or potential shareholder, you are interested in seeing reliable results.

The real value of the auditing process is to ensure shareholders that they can rely on the financial statements issued by management. There is no promise that the statements represent the one absolute correct answer—because there is no such thing.

The Question of Reliability

Every investor who follows the fundamentals wants to believe that financial statements are completely reliable. The truth, in some cases, is more simple. The chief executive officer's (CEO) job might be more easily described as maintaining or improving the price of the company's common stock. If the CEO is given incentives in the form of stock options—rewards for reporting ever-growing profits and profit margins, for example—then the incentives certainly could provide motivation for manipulating what is reported on financial statements. This practice is not necessarily widespread, but it does occur.

✦ KEY POINT

The chief executive officer's job might be to lead operations to ever-increasing profits, or it might be to improve the market value of the stock.

The vast majority of publicly traded companies report with integrity and can be depended on for reliable financial information. The danger arises when investors themselves rely on the wrong information, or invest without thoroughly understanding the nature of information they receive. Some recommendations follow.

- *Never make decisions when you are approached by telephone. Period.* No one is going to solicit your business with a truly good deal. You have to find those on your own.
- *Recognize the narrative sections of annual reports for what they are.* One annual report included current-year losses exceeding previous years'. Even so, the letter from the CEO expressed great optimism: "The reduction in the rate of increases in net losses underscores our move toward the direction of profitability."
- *Watch a company's performance over the long term.* The annual report includes financial statements for the latest year and for the two years preceding (for the balance sheet) and three years preceding (for the statement of income).
- *Identify the causes of wide swings in any accounts on the financial statements.* It should trouble you if a company's operating results swing widely from one year to the next. If you see a history of inconsistent results, you may wonder why. It happens in every company that one-time extraordinary items have to be included.
- *Read the auditor's report.* Finally, read the auditor's report accompanying the financial statement. The auditor's report contains three sections. First is the introductory paragraph, which states that an audit has occurred and identifies responsibilities of management and of the auditor. Second is the scope paragraph, stating that the audit was performed in accordance with generally accepted auditing standards, and that the audit provides a reasonable basis for the opinion. Third is the opinion paragraph, reporting the auditor's professional judgment about the accuracy and fairness of the financial statements. If a fourth paragraph is included, there is a problem. Only when qualifying remarks are required is there a fourth paragraph.

🔑 KEY POINT

The auditor's report should always be read carefully. Any qualifying remarks might be red flags and should not be ignored.

Remember, the statements are management's reports; the auditor only examines them for accuracy and compliance. So when qualifying remarks are found, that provides you with valuable insight and information.

Cooking the Books

How can a financial statement reflect transactions in less than an accurate manner? Investors depend on the independent audit to ensure that a company's financial statements are accurate. But this audit involves much more than just checking to make sure no one is embezzling and that the company has adequate financial controls. Auditing firms look more deeply into the workings of the company to ensure that income, costs, and expenses are posted at the correct time. They also strive to ensure that, in every respect, financial statements present an accurate reflection of what occurred during the year, the valuation of assets and liabilities, and the handling of transactions so that investors can know with a high degree of certainty that the fundamentals are dependable.

Even with the safeguards in place, it is possible to "cook the books." This means that financial statements are altered in some way. Management is under considerable pressure from its board of directors in some cases. From management's point of view, the most desirable yearly result has to do with the marketability of stock, meaning that market price has to be maintained over time. The most obvious reflection of this is profits at a higher level than last year and a consistent net margin. Investors expect this, and so management is pressured to produce desired results. Those desired results do not always come to pass from the results of operations.

As a consequence, a chief financial officer (CFO) or CEO may be tempted to make adjustments in the books so that a desired result will be possible, including higher sales, consistent net margin, or higher net profits than the year before. The pressure is only made worse when analysts in brokerage firms or with research services make predictions based on detailed studies of the company's past financial statements. Those predictions determine whether or not the stock remains in favor. A "buy" recommendation by a brokerage firm may be changed if the company's results don't come out as predicted—even if the final result is still satisfactory based on long-term trends and internal forecasts. So in some respects, outside analysts have a lot to do with the stock's marketability, which also leads to pressure on financial executives to meet those outsiders' expectations.

Historically, audits by the SEC have uncovered some more serious examples of book cooking. A distinction has to be made between interpretation within the rules, and out-and-out cooking of the books. As reported in the June 25, 1984, issue of *Fortune*, "Managers don't have to cook the books to manipulate earnings; they often have all the power they need in the leeway built into accounting rules."

🔑 *KEY POINT*

Financial decisions involve many judgment calls. The financial statement does not represent an absolute "right" or "true" answer, only an interpretation of what occurred during the year.

Certain types of corporations, notably in the financial industry—banks and insurance companies, for example—have considerable leeway in the methods they choose for establishing reserves. While reserves are required by statute, the leeway is to be found in translating from statutory to generally accepted accounting principles (GAAP), a process that takes up considerable time and effort during audits, both on the part of management and the auditing firm. The less reserve a financial services company compiles during the year, the higher the current profits.

The reserve illustration is only one example of how profits can be manipulated, and it is not necessarily dishonest. A reserve requirement may have numerous interpretations, and management might argue that they have the right to place the most favorable interpretation on financial estimates, as long as those estimates fall within the broad guidelines range. Another example may be the deferral of writing off loans that, in fact, will never be collected. When a bank or savings institution underestimates its bad loans, it reduces its bad debt expense (thus, raising profits). The institution also may continue to accrue interest income on those loans, compounding the misleading reportage.

One especially troubling practice is that of attempting to engineer earnings so that profits are reporting consistently, creating the impression of stability. This practice is referred to as banking earnings. In the real world, earnings often occur irregularly and without any dependable consistency. However, management prefers steady growth over the years, so the temptation to bank earnings may lead to some fancy accounting.

Here's how it works. A portion of this year's earnings are deferred until a future period, with some type of justification. Accounting rules require that transactions are to be booked into the correct period. Thus, income should be recognized, or booked, in the year it is earned, even if it is not received until the following year. Costs and expenses are to be recognized in the year incurred, even if not paid until the following year. This practice accurately reflects the true status of business as of the end of the period, assuming that all income, costs, and expenses are truly recognized in their earned or accrued period. This system is referred to as accrual basis accounting. Figure 3.1 summarizes the way it works.

FIGURE 3.1 The Accrual System

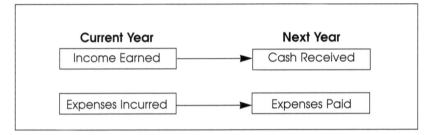

The problem with this accounting system is that it can be complicated—not in the mechanical or procedural sense, but in the discretionary sense. When is income actually earned? In some instances, arguments can be made to record income immediately or to spread it over time. The motive should be to apply a consistent principle, but in practice the accrual system provides some flexibility to management, often enough flexibility to create the appearance of a very smooth and consistent income level year after year.

✎ KEY POINT

The accrual system is the most accurate because it recognizes transactions in the correct period. It also complicates matters and provides more flexibility in interpretation of the numbers.

Deferral of earnings, or banking, is only one method used by some financial managers. Another involves changing of accounting methods or estimates. For example, a corporation estimates a reserve for bad debts, intended to allow for future accounts receivable that will not be collected. A lot of discretion may be available in the method chosen for establishing the reserve. In this area of accounting—estimating—a lot of discretion is allowed. Thus, in a particularly good year, it will be tempting to establish a larger than necessary reserve estimate. It can be reduced in future periods, when actual results are not as good. This practice creates a different kind of reserve, called the "sugar bowl."

It is not just exceptionally large earnings that are deferred for later use. Perhaps more troubling is the practice of deferring the reporting of large losses. For example, a corporation may know it has to take a write-off on a subsidiary investment that has lost money. It might defer booking the loss for a year or more, however, which artificially creates the impression that the corporation is continuing on a profitable course. When corporations buy assets, those assets are always booked at cost value. So if the asset is worth considerably more several years later, that fact is not usually acknowledged—at least not until the asset is sold and a big profit is realized. This can work in reverse as well. Let's say a company invests in an asset that subsequently loses value. If the corporation keeps the asset on its books at original cost, deferring the sale because it doesn't want to report the loss, that is a form of deferring bad news. When assets are kept longer than it makes sense so that losses are not reported, it can also eventually result in larger losses.

Overcoming the Problem

The question of reliability has to be addressed by the fundamental analyst. At the very least, you have to expect accurate information. Because each financial statement tends to be outdated by the time it is issued, you depend on long-term information—trends established over time—to make informed decisions. If those trends are artificially created in an accounting department within the corporation, how can you make an informed decision?

It helps to remember the primary role of the SEC to oversee the securities industry and to ensure that the market operates in a fair and orderly manner. Its objective is to protect the investing public. That means you have a right to full disclosure of information. This concept is most often applied to new public offerings and to information provided in an offering prospectus; but the principle also has application to the methods used for reporting financial transactions in any publicly listed corporation.

🗝 *KEY POINT*

The role of the regulatory system is to protect investors. It cannot provide an ironclad guarantee that financial statements are absolutely true and correct.

Depending on the extensive accounting regulatory system is one way to assure yourself that the markets are efficient, not only as a market-place, but in terms of disclosure. A second method is to study financial information over a number of years. The two trends to look out for appear to contradict one another. You should be suspicious when a company's financial results swing wildly from excessive profits to deep losses. Such a company is not being well-managed and growth is occurring in an out-of-control environment. That should not be seen as a situation appropriate for long-term investing. Equally suspicious is the company whose earnings rise almost predictably on the same course each and every year; whose profit margins are generally within a narrow range every year; and whose other fundamentals follow a straight-line trend—to a fault. In reality, such dependability is rare or nonexistent. In such a case, there is a good chance that some account-ing manipulation is taking place.

If you have invested in the stock of a company and its fundamentals are predictable, perhaps even boring, the question you need to ask is: If the company is manipulating the financial results, is that a bad thing? From the point of view of an investor, you might realize that to a degree, managing the timing of income may have a positive effect on the stock price without materially affecting the true results. Because the leeway is provided, management has considerable discretion in how and when it recognizes transactions, values inventories, and establishes its reserves. The truth is, as long as no one is defrauded or otherwise damaged, it is unlikely that the practice will be considered a violation of the rules and regulations.

Accounting is not precise. It is so highly regulated and requires such time and effort because of its complexity. The practice of banking earn-ings usually is motivated by the desire to bring order to a chaotic world, rather than being intended to defraud or deceive anyone.

✦ KEY POINT

No one really knows where the line is between discretionary accounting decision making and misrepresentation. It appears that the line may be in one place or another, depending on whether or not anyone is damaged.

Trusting the Fundamentals

With the observation that accounting has many variables, you might wonder whether financial statements can be trusted. People tend to believe that a published, audited statement is the last word and in many respects it is. Having gone through the internal systems, independent audits, and oversight by the SEC, a published financial statement probably is as accurate as it can be. Remember that the fundamental analyst is a long-term thinker. Thus, you should not be preoccupied with momentary changes: stock price changes, rumors or gossip, or exceptionally high reports of transactions, especially those involving one-time write-offs or other changes materially affecting results. Think long-term. This thinking makes sense in the supply and demand environment of the market, where technical indicators rule the thinking of most people (i.e., the Dow Jones Industrial Average).

Long-term thinking also applies to financial statements and the dependability of financial information. Let's assume that in its latest financial statement a company made certain accounting decisions that do not completely disclose matters. Chances are good that the changes will be absorbed in coming years, for better or worse, and that the tinkering will have a short-term effect. If you are able to overcome the tendency most investors have to think short term, and become a long-term thinker, then what does it matter? Most of the accrual adjustments made by companies to interpret the treatment of income, costs, and expenses, have consequences in only two years: the current year and the year following. Thus, interpretive decisions are short term in nature and, in truth, may do much to maintain your investment's value. It is important to keep in mind the way the market thinks. Short-term indicators rule. So if the analyst of a large brokerage house says your company will have a net margin of 11 percent, and it comes in at 10.25 percent, the stock price may tumble. It will probably recover the following quarter so it does not really matter in terms of long-term value.

> ### ✦ KEY POINT
>
> Accounting adjustments—even if inaccurate this year—usually are short term in nature and most likely will be absorbed within one year. As long-term thinkers, it may be misguided to assign too much concern to short-term management accounting policies.

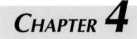

CHAPTER 4

Financial Reporting— How They Do It

*B*asic financial statements conform to a universal format, making it fairly easy to become familiar with them and to identify key fundamental elements. Many accounting conventions are purposely conservative so that the opportunities to distort financial statements are limited.

As an example of the conservative approach, assets are always included at cost. So even if an asset has increased in value significantly, that will not be reflected in the asset listing. Current market values of real estate often are substantially higher than the values shown in financial statements, not only as a result of inflation, but due to depreciation as well. The company writes off a portion of a building's value over time, so rather than showing an increase in investment value reflecting the true market situation, financial statement rules mandate that the reported value of real assets decline over time.

Extreme distortions between reported asset value and current market value will be included in the notes of the financial statement. These notes contain much valuable and important information, not only about assets but about all segments of the financial statement. You do not need to take a course in accounting or bookkeeping in order to understand what is included in the corporate financial statement. There are no special secrets known only to accountants; the format and rules of reporting are fairly simple and easy to follow.

Financial Statement Basics

There are three basic financial statements: (1) the balance sheet, (2) the statement of income, and (3) the statement of cash flow. Further information is found in any supplemental schedules (providing greater detail for specific accounts where needed), the auditor's report, and the all-important notes to the financial statements. As described below, each financial statement serves a specific purpose and provides you with important information that can be used to better make investment decisions.

The Balance Sheet

The first financial statement is the balance sheet. This statement reports the dollar value of accounts as of a specified date, usually the end of the latest fiscal year or the end of the most recent fiscal quarter. The reporting date of the balance sheet corresponds with the ending date of the period reported in the statement of income. (For example, the statement of income will report transactions from January 1 through December 31; the accompanying balance sheet reports balances as of December 31.)

Assets.   There are three sections to the balance sheet. The first is assets. These are the dollar values of valuables the company owns (such as bank accounts, inventories, and assets) and accounts due from others. Assets owned by the organization are further divided into subclassifications based on the type of asset. This subdividing becomes important in fundamental analysis because many trends and ratios you will use depend on distinctions between different types of accounts.

The first three groups are tangible assets. The first group—and the one that is always listed first on the balance sheet—is current assets. These are called current because they are readily available to the organization to fund operations. Current assets include the dollar balances of all cash accounts; accounts receivable (the total of all outstanding accounts, less a reserve for bad debts); dollar value of inventory on hand; and other current assets, including marketable securities, notes receivable, and other accounts that can be converted to cash within one year.

The second group within the assets section is noncurrent assets. These are also called fixed assets and represent assets that are depreciated over many years (rather than being treated as current-year expenses). All property, plant, and equipment are included in this section. When a company purchases a capital asset, such as real estate, machinery and equipment, autos and trucks, or office furniture, such an asset cannot be treated as a business expense in the year purchased. Instead, it is set up as an asset and depreciated over a number of years. So the company takes a deduction for depreciation each year until the value of the asset is fully depreciated. (For many corporations, depreciation may also be listed as amortization and/or depletion.) Depreciation recovery periods, as they are called, may last between 3 and 32 years or longer, depending on the type of asset involved. Long-term assets are subtotaled and then reduced by the value of an account called accumulated depreciation. In this way, the dollar value of all long-term assets is reduced by the amount of depreciation claimed over the years. Eventually, all assets subject to depreciation are reduced to a zero balance. Land investments are reported in a separate category from real estate improvements, because land is not subject to depreciation.

The next group is called deferred assets. Deferrals are expenses that apply to the following period, and will be reassigned as expenses in the following year.

The fourth group is called intangible assets. These are assets that have no physical value. For example, some companies acquire subsidiaries and assign a goodwill value to the name; that would qualify as an intangible asset. (If you acquired rights to the brand name "Oreo," you would have a tasty intangible asset because buyers ask for the product by name.) Goodwill is the amount paid in an acquisition above a company's book value. In other cases, a company may acquire a contractual right upon buying up another business. The seller agrees not to open a competing business within a specified number of years. While it is possible that no money exchanged hands, this contractual agreement has value (lowered competition and customer loyalty from previous owner), so an intangible asset called a "covenant not to compete" may be established. In calculating book value per share, intangible assets are excluded—the total of assets to be used in the calculation are reduced by the assigned dollar value of intangible assets.

Assets are added together and the total is reported on one line on the balance sheet. The sum of all liabilities and shareholders' equity will add up to the same dollar amount as total assets.

Liabilities. The second of three sections of the balance sheet is liabilities, the obligations owed by the company. These are divided into groups that always are listed in the same order.

The first group in this section is current portion of long-term debt (current liabilities). These are liabilities that will be paid within the coming 12 months. Included are accounts payable (amounts due to vendors); taxes payable (to local, state, and federal agencies for payroll and other taxes); and 12 months' worth of payments on any loans or notes outstanding.

Current liabilities are distinguished in this manner for a very important reason. One of the most important fundamental tests involves comparisons between current assets and current liabilities (more on those tests in later chapters). The net difference between current assets and liabilities is called working capital.

The next group is long-term liabilities, which includes all debts payable beyond the coming 12 months. Important fundamental tests and ratios involve comparisons between long-term debt and equity. These two together are broadly referred to in fundamental analysis as a company's capitalization.

The final group is deferred credits. These amounts represent income that will be recorded in a future year, being held, or deferred, in the current year. They are not true liabilities, but income owed to a future year. Companies may receive income payments in advance of their earned period, so they are listed along with liabilities, to be reversed and transferred to income when they become earned.

Shareholders' equity.   The third section of the balance sheet is shareholders' equity. As the name implies, this is the value of the company. It consists of the difference between assets (what is owned) and liabilities (what is owed). Shareholders' equity is divided into two primary groups.

First is capital stock, which is the dollar amount of shares outstanding as of the time they were issued and sold, plus any additional paid-in capital, and less any adjustments. Second is retained earnings, which represents all profits from past years reduced by payments of taxes and dividends paid to stockholders.

The relationship between the sections of the balance sheet is shown in Figure 4.1.

Figure 4.1 shows the format normally used for the preparation of the balance sheet. This is, however, the most basic form. Most corporate

FIGURE 4.1 The Balance Sheet

```
                        Company Name
                        Balance Sheet
                     December 31, ____

Current Assets:
   Cash                                    xxx,xxx
   Accounts Receivable                     xxx,xxx
   Inventory                               xxx,xxx

   Total Current Assets                    xxx,xxx

Noncurrent Assets:
   Real Estate                             xxx,xxx
   Equipment                               xxx,xxx
   Automotive                              xxx,xxx
   Subtotal                                xxx,xxx
   Less: Accumulated Depreciation        – xxx,xxx

   Net Noncurrent Assets                   xxx,xxx

Total Assets                             x,xxx,xxx   ◄──────┐
                                                            │
Current Liabilities:                                        │
   Accounts Payable                        xxx,xxx          │
   Taxes Payable                           xxx,xxx          │
   Notes Payable                           xxx,xxx          │
                                                            │
   Total Current Liabilities               xxx,xxx          │
                                                            │
Noncurrent Liabilities                     xxx,xxx          │
                                                            │
Total Liabilities                          xxx,xxx          │
                                                            │
Shareholders' Equity:                                       │
   Capital Stock                           xxx,xxx          │
   Retained Earnings                       xxx,xxx          │
   Total Net Worth                         xxx,xxx          │
                                                            │
Total Liabilities and Shareholders' Equity  x,xxx,xxx  ◄───┘
```

⚷ KEY POINT

The balance sheet is a summary of account balances as of a single date, which is the end of the latest reporting period.

balance sheets are comparative, showing the balances for the current year as well as the prior year. Many further break down results for different subsidiary companies.

Shareholders' equity is normally reported in a separate statement, and this may be considered a fourth financial statement by itself. However, the separate report actually is a detailed breakdown of shareholders' equity as reported on the balance sheet.

Notes may be referenced and included to explain certain important features for particular accounts. Finally, many additional details may be provided with supplementary schedules, breaking down and elaborating on the balances in accounts receivable (including aging of accounts and a detailed description of the reserve for bad debts), long-term assets, liabilities, and shareholders' equity.

The Statement of Income

The second financial statement is the statement of income (see Figure 4.2). This is the statement that shows the results of operations over a period of time, usually a full year or the latest quarter. The statement of income is also called the profit and loss statement (or P&L).

The statement of income is divided into several distinct groups. At the top is the total of sales or revenues for the period being reported. This may be shown as a single line item (gross sales), a detailed breakdown by product or service area, or a gross amount reduced by returns and allowances (net sales).

Next is a group called cost of sales. This includes all costs directly associated with the production of sales (as opposed to expenses that cannot be directly assigned). (Rent, for example, will not rise or fall as sales rise or fall, so it is an expense rather than a cost.) The cost of sales usually is reported as a single line, and is subtracted from sales or revenues. Total cost of goods sold is subtracted from sales to arrive at the period's gross profit.

The next group involves some breakdown of selling, general, and administrative expenses. Some companies make a distinction between

FIGURE 4.2   The Statement of Income

Company Name	
Statement of Income	
For the Fiscal Year Ending December 31, ____	
Gross Sales	$ x,xxx,xxx
Less: Returns and Allowances	– x,xxx
Net Sales	$ x,xxx,xxx
Cost of Sales	– x,xxx,xxx
Gross Profit	$ x,xxx,xxx
General, Selling, and Administrative Expenses (Schedule I)	– x,xxx,xxx
Operating Profit	$ xx,xxx
Plus: Other Income	xx,xxx
Less: Other Expenses	– xx,xxx
Pretax Profit	$ xxx,xxx
Less: Federal Income Taxes	– xx,xxx
Net Profit	$ xxx,xxx

selling and general expenses; others have one section for all expenses without making a distinction. If the list is extensive, the details are provided in a supplementary schedule and only a single-line total is included on the financial statement itself.

When all expenses are subtracted from the gross profit, the remaining value is operating profit. Adjustments are made to this for other income and expense, meaning nonoperating transactions. These may include interest income or expense, or profit or loss from foreign currency exchange, for example. After these adjustments are made, the remaining value is pretax profit. This is not the true bottom line, however. The company probably owes income taxes on its profits, so tax liability is deducted to arrive at net profit. In the interest of consistency in comparisons, the actual net profit should be used for all ratio analysis calling for net profit. A word of caution, however: The terminology suggested here is not used universally. In some instances, net profit might refer to operating profit without adjusting for other income or expense, and without calculating income tax liabilities. You should ensure that your own analysis is consistent between companies; adjustments might be necessary if and when the same terms or definitions are not being used.

Like the balance sheet, this statement of income is highly simplified. Companies report in comparative form, showing results for three successive years, often including percentages from sales (100 percent) down to the bottom line, or with breakdowns by major subsidiary operations.

✦ KEY POINT

The statement of income summarizes the transactions over a period, such as one full year or the latest quarter. For consistency and uniformity in reporting, the ending date of that period corresponds to the date reported on the balance sheet.

The Statement of Cash Flow

The third and last financial statement is the statement of cash flow (see Figure 4.3), also referred to as the cash flow statement. This statement shows where a company received cash, and where it spent cash, summarizing the difference for the fiscal year.

The fiscal year by the statement always corresponds to the fiscal year covered by the statement of income, ending with the date of the balance sheet. The statement is important because it shows where the money came from and where it went—in other words, it is a summary of cash flow for the year. Working capital—the net difference between current assets and current liabilities—defines the company's cash-based health in the sense that cash and accounts that are converted to cash in the near future are requirements for smooth operations. Current bills have to be paid, including payroll and other expenses. This means that inventory

FIGURE 4.3   The Statement of Cash Flow

Company Name
Statement of Cash Flow
For the Fiscal Year Ending December 31, ____

Cash Was Provided by:

Net Profit	$xxx,xxx
Plus: Noncash Expenses	xx,xxx
Adjusted Net Profit	xxx,xxx
Proceeds from the Sale of Capital Assets	xxx,xxx
Loan Proceeds Received	xxx,xxx
Total Provisions of Funds	$xxx,xxx

Cash Was Used in:

Repayment of Loans and Notes	$xxx,xxx
Retirement of Bonds	xxx,xxx
Dividends Paid to Stockholders	xxx,xxx
Purchase of Capital Assets	xxx,xxx
Total Uses of Funds	$xxx,xxx

Net Increase (Decrease) in Funds $xxx,xxx ←┐

Changes in Working Capital:

	Beginning Balance	Ending Balance	Change
Cash	$xx,xxx	$xx,xxx	$xx,xxx
Accounts Receivable	xx,xxx	xx,xxx	xx,xxx
Inventory	xx,xxx	xx,xxx	xx,xxx
Accounts Payable	xx,xxx	xx,xxx	xx,xxx
Taxes Payable	xx,xxx	xx,xxx	xx,xxx
Notes Payable	$xx,xxx	$xx,xxx	$xx,xxx
Net Changes in Working Capital			$xx,xxx ←┘

levels have to be maintained intelligently, accounts have to be collected, and management has to plan ahead. When a company's cash flow is poor, it is a sign of trouble. So a careful analysis of cash flow is a good fundamental indicator of how well management has planned ahead, uses its resources, and controls current assets.

The statement contains three groups. The first shows how cash was provided; from operations, from loan proceeds, or from the sale of capital assets (plant and equipment). The second group shows how cash was used (for repayment of liabilities, the purchase of capital assets (plant and equipment), or payment of shareholders' dividends, for example). The third group is a summary of changes in working capital (balance changes in current assets and current liabilities from the beginning of the year to the end of the year).

🏃 KEY POINT

The statement of cash flow shows where funds came from and how they were applied. It shows you how a company manages its cash and funds operations.

The statement of cash flow tells the fundamental analyst how well management has planned its cash flow for the year, controlled cash and other current assets, and funded its operations. Just as it reflects poorly on management if cash flow is poor, an excess of liquid assets can also indicate problems. Some examples make the point.

Example: One large corporation had more than $5 million on hand through the year. While operations required large amounts of cash, the balance was excessive. The company also carried nearly $3 million in short-term debt with a relatively high rate of interest. The interest expense could have been eliminated if a portion of available and excess cash had been spent to pay off those obligations.

Example: A corporation recently went through a rapid growth period. As one of the signs of this growth, outstanding accounts receivable balances have risen. While sales volume is higher, the rate of increase in receivables outpaced the rate of sales growth. As a consequence, less cash is available for funding current operations. The company tightened up its collection policies only after realizing that the longer accounts remained outstanding, the higher the rate of bad debts.

Example: A company has too much inventory. Current stock of raw materials includes many obsolete items that should be removed. Excessive inventory means higher storage and rental expenses, higher insurance premiums, more field management time and difficulty in locating inventory for shipping, and less efficiency—not to mention that cash is tied up unnecessarily, affecting the company's ability to efficiently fund operations.

The statement of cash flow demonstrates management's consistency in managing problems like these. It also shows how, even when profits are up, cash flow can be marginal or poor. One of the greatest threats to a corporation's financial health is poor cash flow. Ironically, during periods of rapid growth, the greatest problem faced by companies is worsening cash flow. (The company may need to buy inventory or raw materials to meet demand, but collections lag behind expenses.) So the statement of cash flow is of critical importance, especially to smaller aggressive growth stocks.

The three financial statements are tied together in specific ways. Net profit is added to retained earnings each year, increasing the equity of the company. (Or, in years where a loss occurs, retained earnings and shareholders' equity are reduced.) Net profit is also the starting point on the sources of funds in the statement of cash flow. And changes in working capital also correspond to changes in current assets and current liabilities reported on the balance sheet. The interrelationship of the three financial statements is summarized in Figure 4.4.

FIGURE 4.4 Financial Statements: How They Tie Together

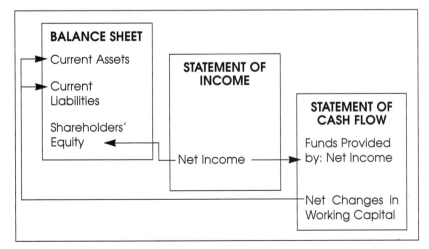

Judging a Company's Financial Health

Your task as your own fundamental analyst is to determine the financial health of a company—whether you are thinking of buying, holding, or selling a stock. The financial statements of the company serve as your basic documents for making this judgment. However, financial health might have several different definitions. To be accurate in your judgment, you need to make comparisons, and you also need to ensure that your comparisons are applied fairly in each case.

So how do you define a financially healthy company? Some standard methods for applying this definition include the following:

Increases in sales volume.   People usually assume that a growing company is a healthy company. While this is true, you also need to ensure that a company is growing in the right way. One of the more popular and standardized tests is the dollar amount of sales from one year to another. Most people, when thinking of growth in corporate terms, first think of total sales as the best measure. However, this is a troubling indicator when looked at in isolation. Growth by itself is not necessarily a positive sign; in fact, growth can do a lot of damage to a company's financial health if not properly controlled. What good are increased sales if the amount and yield of net sales are falling? You also need to know the cause of sales volume in order to understand its significance. If volume growth results solely from new acquisitions, it is not growth at all, but merely a reconfiguration of the base. Volume growth due to more unit sales or higher prices has an entirely different interpretation.

➤ *KEY POINT*

The importance of ever-growing sales volume receives too much emphasis. If overly rapid expansion results in a cash flow crisis, the sales increase is not good for the company's long-term health.

Growth in sales volume *and* net margin.   A more accurate measure of health is a combination of sales volume and net margin. In other words, if sales are increasing each year while the net margin (percentage of net sales to total sales) remains at the same level or within a reasonable range, this is healthy growth. If sales volume and net margin are coordinated in this manner—especially if cash flow continues to be carefully controlled by management—then a good growth pattern emerges and the company can be considered fiscally healthy.

Growth in net profit dollar amount.   Another popular but misleading way to measure growth is by looking only at the dollar amount of net profits. It is far more important to be aware of net margin than the dollar amount of sales. For example, look at the following pattern of sales and profits, along with the net margin:

Year	Sales	Profits	Net Margin
1	$14,633,200	$1,536,500	10.5%
2	17,561,000	1,740,200	9.9
3	21,080,600	1,877,400	8.9
4	26,993,400	2,174,300	8.1
5	31,003,100	2,241,900	7.2

Note that while profits are rising each year along with growth in sales volume, the net margin is falling. Such a trend is troubling. It shows that management is not able to properly maintain its relative yield with growth. So a growth in net profits alone can be deceiving.

Competitive position.   If the company you are considering has competitors within its industry, a good way to measure its health is by comparing all of the fundamentals to those of its competitors—not once, but as a series of relative trends. You will be able to spot emerging new leaders and the gradual decline of older ones by watching how the fundamentals change—sales volume, net margin, asset strength, and other tests. In applying fundamental tests to a company, comparisons to other companies in the same industry are highly useful, because all competitors are subject to the same economic influences in the same way. For example, a company whose operations are sensitive to rising interest rates shares that characteristic with all other companies in its industry.

Assets and shareholders' equity.   Some fiscal health can be measured in terms of book value. As a company grows and accumulates profit, it should also be able to reduce its relative share of debt, increase the value of its assets, and gain financial strength overall. If a company experiences growth but loses shareholders' equity, then it is probably depending too heavily on debt capital, or failing to manage cash flow adequately. Higher profits are not worth the effort if they result in endangering the future financial strength of the organization.

Capitalization mix. Corporations capitalize their growth through a combination of methods. Shareholders, of course, buy shares of stock and provide the corporation with equity capital. Corporations also may borrow money through notes and loans or by issuing bonds. These are forms of debt capital and must be repaid with interest, which reduces net income. Equity capital, in comparison, may or may not be compensated through dividend payments. The mix of capital is an important test, not just of growth, but how growth is achieved. If a corporation becomes excessively dependent on debt capital, it may erode current and future earnings through ever-increasing interest expense.

Dividend rate. The fundamentalist is always aware of yield and, to some degree, technicians also appreciate the significance of high-yielding stocks. A corporation's health often is judged by the consistency of dividend payments, the steady or increasing rate of payment, and the significance of any reductions in rate or even skipped dividends.

Stock price. Ultimately, the majority of individual investors, including all technicians, judge a company's health by how well its stock price moves upward or, equally important, how well it holds its value when the rest of the market is falling. Stock price reflects demand and a perception of potential growth for the company, so a stock's price strength does reflect what the market believes about the company. You will discover that companies with strong fundamentals (sales volume, net margin, dividend payment rates, asset strength, and price-earnings ratio) also tend to have more stability in stock price.

The Annual Report

One of the strangest documents in the stock market has to be the annual report. This is a very expensively produced, often multiple-color report including financial statements and forecasts, a message from the top management, photographs, descriptions of the operations of the company, and other interesting information. Most of it is strictly promotional.

Annual reports are useful for finding out about the industry or industries the company is involved in, and in learning about products or services it manufactures or sells. But you are not likely to read an annual report that has any bad news whatsoever. (Even bad news will be reported in terms that makes it sound very good.) Annual reports usually are produced by a company's public relations department or an outside advertising agency. The message from the president is rarely written by the president, but is instead the best possible spin put on everything the company does. ("The past is a strong indicator, we have had a record year, and the future is very exciting.") The document also presents information with colorful, 3-D graphs and offers the reader a slogan that often sounds good but says little or nothing: "Leading the way to tomorrow" or "On the edge of discovery" or "Leadership that cares about you."

So why do companies go through the exercise? Because the annual report is required by law (the financial—not the promotional—part). Publicly traded companies have to publish financial statements in a prescribed form, containing disclosures of all important information including an auditor's report. As financial statements are published as a part of the annual report, these documents certainly are handy. They can be requested from the corporate headquarters directly, by mail, telephone, over the Internet, or they can be picked up from a brokerage firm. As a convenient way to find the financial statement, annual reports serve a worthwhile purpose. However, you can also glean additional information from the annual report. Don't forget that the primary purpose of the annual report—beyond compliance with the law—is to recruit new shareholders, impress analysts, and outshine competitors.

A company's management realizes that the majority of investors do not spend a lot of time studying financial statements, even when they recognize their significance. People simply don't like to spend time with numbers. So documents like the prospectus, annual report, and forms filed with the Securities and Exchange Commission rarely are read as carefully as they deserve. Instead, most people prefer to read the sections of the annual report that avoid the numbers and provide the reader with color pictures and promising narratives.

⚷ KEY POINT

Don't forget that a company's annual report is a glossy promotional piece. Read the whole thing carefully, but watch the tone and compare them from year to year to see what is really going on in a company.

What should you look for in this document? First of all, don't make the common mistake of looking only at one result—sales or profits, for example. Identify those indicators that make up your overall fundamental analysis program, and then test them against what is reported in the financial sections of the annual report.

Read the notes completely.   The notes to the financial statements may contain important financial information. For example, you may learn of pending lawsuits, labor problems, changes in management, or accounting method changes (more on notes in the next chapter).

Read the auditor's report.   Has the independent auditing firm issued an unqualified report? If not, what reasons are provided for qualifying the report? Any qualifying remarks should lead to further questioning and investigation.

Look for extraordinary items.   The company's financial results will be distorted if any extraordinary items are included, such as a write-off of a subsidiary loss, large adjustments for international exchange rate losses or gains, or changes in accounting methods. Those items should be discounted when performing any ongoing trend analysis. If extraordinary items show up frequently on the financial statements, you should start to wonder why.

Read the management's analysis of financial results.
The annual report always contains a message from the president or chief executive officer (CEO), including an analysis of financial results. If the results are poor, you should be interested in seeing how the CEO deals with it. For example, let's say the company's sales are down and the financials show a net loss. Here are two possible ways a CEO might discuss these results:

1. Putting a positive spin on it:

    We are very pleased with the promising results of operations for the current year. Our limited net losses reflect intentional regrouping among our subsidiary operations as we invest today's resources in the development of future profits. The continuing strong performance in our primary product line supports this intentional short-term strategy.

2. Confronting the problem directly:

    We show a net loss for the year. This resulted from poor performance among several subsidiary operations and is not expected to repeat in future years. We intend to prevent future losses by selling off unprofitable subsidiary operations, and have taken action to divest ourselves of these divisions as quickly as possible. Meanwhile, profits from our primary product line remain strong.

You can conclude for yourself what the numbers reveal and the CEO's explanation (or spin) on those results tells you not only how or why the losses occurred, but what steps, if any, are being taken to correct any deficiencies in management strategy. Perhaps most important of all, the approach taken in the annual report displays the company's integrity and willingness to speak to its shareholders about the good and the bad.

✳ KEY POINT

With clever writing, even the worst news can be made to sound positive. Look at the numbers carefully. Read explanations not to get financial information, but to draw conclusions about management's integrity in the way it communicates with its shareholders.

To begin researching a company through a study of its annual report, apply the basic rule of fundamental analysis: Never look at only one year. Contact the company's investor relations department and ask for copies of the current annual report, plus the last three or four. See how the communication of financial information varies from one year to the next. Has the top management changed? If so, why? Has the sales and profit picture changed? Is the capitalization improving or depending more on debt than equity? Do each year's forecasts come to pass, or are they largely inflated? By looking at the annual reports over several years, you will get a better picture of matters than you will from financial statements alone.

Also be aware that when the numbers look bad, some companies try to focus on other matters: the social value of their products, their concern for their employees and customers, or their dedication to quality. When this occurs, look at the numbers more carefully. Read the notes and the auditor's report. Make sure that you can tell what is going on, not only by what the numbers show, but also by what the CEO's letter says, how it is said, and what it does not say.

The Prospectus

Another document you should become familiar with is the offering prospectus. This document is intended to disclose everything you need to know about a company going public, including financial statements, a discussion of the risks of investing, the nature of the business in which the company engages, and its management.

The prospectus is especially important to you if you are considering buying shares in a corporation going public for the first time. That is called an initial public offering (IPO). Read this document carefully, and compare IPO prospectus documents for several companies before deciding whether or not one is a good deal. Be aware, too, that when you invest in an IPO, dilution will occur. That means that the book value per share will drop. The more shares sold, the lower the book value per share for all shareholders. Make comparisons to determine the degree of dilution. By comparing, you will find that some stock prices are more inflated than others, meaning you take greater risks investing in highly diluted IPOs. In some carefully crafted deals, new shareholders can suffer very high dilution immediately, while existing shareholders' share value rises, because as a new investor, you would be asked to pay a per-share price higher than existing shareholders' current share value. This would not be a good deal.

Also check the section of the prospectus called "use of proceeds" or "use of offering proceeds." The prospectus discloses how much of the money being raised will be paid in commissions to the underwriters of the offering; for transfer payments to previous owners (in other words, when new shareholders buy out previous shareholders), and other fees not going directly into corporate management. Calculate the percentage of the total offering going to fees and expenses, dividends, and buy-outs of previous shareholders. Compare between IPOs to determine which are the higher-cost deals. Disclosure is required, but you have to read the disclosures to find out how proceeds will be used. You might discover, for example, that the corporation intends to pay off old debts or reward its executive officers or preferred shareholders with high dividends.

Take the one action that most investors and would-be investors don't take. Read the prospectus. You may even contact the corporation and ask for the more detailed 10K, a report that is filed with the SEC each year. Remember, the prospectus and the 10K alone don't tell the whole story. You are ultimately responsible for comparative fundamental analysis; developing information for decision making, and determining

🔑 *KEY POINT*

Make sure that when buying stock as part of an IPO, you are not merely bailing out the company's existing shareholders or paying big dividends to someone else.

how much risk you want to assume. Also remember that the SEC may audit a company's books, but it does not audit the prospectus or the offering terms.

As you read the prospectus, pause at the cover and carefully read the warning the company is required to place there. It has meaning and importance, and should be remembered by every investor thinking about investing in an IPO.

An investment in the securities offered hereby involves a high degree of risk. These securities have not been approved or disapproved by the Securities and Exchange Commission nor has the commission passed upon the accuracy or adequacy of this prospectus. Any representation to the contrary is a criminal offense.

CHAPTER 5

Picking Apart the Financials —Easier Than You Think

*I*dentifying the appropriate methods for performing your own fundamental analysis can and should be a straightforward process. The calculation of formulas is not always necessary. You can get many popular fundamental tests from published sources. The most popular, the price-earnings (PE) ratio, is listed in most financial papers on a daily basis. However, you should understand not only the elements of a formula but the meaning of the results.

What Financial Statements Really Show

Financial statements prepared by generally accepted accounting principles (GAAP) use many safeguards to ensure complete accuracy. Routines important to ensuring the integrity of financial statements are

- bookkeeping procedures to ensure against fraud or inaccuracy;
- checks and balances to prevent any one employee from exercising too much individual discretion;
- requirements for documentation through invoices, receipts, vouchers, and statements;
- approval procedures in advance of payments;
- procedures for handling receipts to ensure proper safeguards; and
- review and approval procedures through internal auditing departments.

🔑 *KEY POINT*

The combination of internal audits, external audits, and regulatory oversight ensures that the quality of financial information is as high as you can reasonably expect.

In sum, these safeguards and procedures, while time-consuming and labor-intensive, ensure that by the time financial statements are published, they have gone through numerous internal control procedures. One of the functions of an independent audit is to review all of these procedures to make sure they are adequate.

The first important test that should be included in every fundamental analysis program is the current ratio. This ratio tests a company's working capital by comparing current assets and liabilities. To compute, divide total current assets by total current liabilities. Expressed in the form of comparative factors, the minimum acceptable current ratio in most cases is 2-to-1 or better. (The current ratio is one of the few tests having a minimum.) The formula for finding a current ratio is summarized in Figure 5.1.

This is one of the universal tests that should always be applied to the latest financial statement. As a general rule, if a company's current ratio falls below 2-to-1, it may be a danger signal. The current ratio, like most tests, should never be the sole test of a company's financial

FIGURE 5.1   Current Ratio (rounded to one decimal)

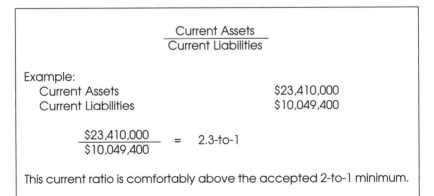

$$\frac{\text{Current Assets}}{\text{Current Liabilities}}$$

Example:
Current Assets $23,410,000
Current Liabilities $10,049,400

$$\frac{\$23,410,000}{\$10,049,400} = 2.3\text{-to-}1$$

This current ratio is comfortably above the accepted 2-to-1 minimum.

strength, but should be reviewed as a part of a larger fundamental analysis.

The 2-to-1 rule does not always apply. In many industries, a company may exhibit a current ratio of 1-to-4 (an inverse ratio, or one with a negative first factor), yet still have excellent financial strength. The attributes of a specific product or service line have much more to do with financial strength than a generalized rule, so application of current ratio should always be done in comparative form—to prior periods as well as to competitor companies in the same industry—and always in combination with other fundamental tests.

✦ KEY POINT

The current ratio is a standard test that should be included in your program—but never as the sole test of a company's financial strength.

Some problems that the current ratio might not reveal or worse, might mask, include that of excessive current assets. When companies have too much cash on hand, that means they may be managed poorly. Perhaps the cash should be used to pay down liabilities and reduce interest expense, for example. If a company's outstanding accounts receivable are too high based on sales levels, or if it is taking too long to collect outstanding accounts, that will artificially inflate current ratio without revealing the serious problem. And if inventory levels are too high, that can also point to problems in managing working capital, but it will not show up in the current ratio.

A variation of the current ratio is the quick assets ratio, also called the acid test. This is identical to the current ratio with one important exception: inventory is excluded. This test is appropriate when a company, by the nature of its business, does not have any inventory (a financial services company, for example), or when inventory tends to be so long-term that the current ratio is distorted. The general standard calls for a quick assets ratio of 1-to-1 or better.

The formula for the quick assets ratio is summarized in Figure 5.2.

In the figure, the quick assets ratio is 1.1-to-1. It surpasses the minimum test that current assets should equal current liabilities (1-to-1).

FIGURE 5.2 Quick Assets Ratio (rounded to one decimal)

$$\frac{\text{Current Assets} - \text{Inventory}}{\text{Current Liabilities}}$$

Example:
Current Assets	$23,410,000
Inventory	$11,943,800
Current Liabilities	$10,049,400

$$\frac{\$23,410,000 - \$11,943,800}{\$10,049,400} = \text{1.1-to-1}$$

This ratio should be thought of as a supplement to the current ratio, to be used only in comparing balance sheets of companies that do not carry inventory on the books due to the nature of the business.

In addition to overall working capital ratios, the specific categories should be tested as well. Accounts receivable and inventory tests will reveal a lot about how the company manages working capital, especially during growth periods. As a company's business expands, the tendency to lose control over working capital becomes a threat to profits and in some instances, to the health of the entire operation.

More detailed examples of worthwhile ratios are provided in later chapters. You may want to concentrate specifically on accounts receivable and inventory tests. By carefully watching the trends in the components making up current assets, you will be able to develop a clear picture broader than that provided just by the current assets ratio.

A second balance sheet ratio of utmost importance in fundamental analysis is the debt/equity ratio shown in Figure 5.3. This ratio shows the percentage of capitalization coming from debt rather than from equity. For example, if the corporation is becoming increasingly dependent on borrowed money rather than on equity capital, that trend will erode profits. The ratio is calculated by dividing total liabilities by tangible net worth (net worth less any intangible assets).

The debt/equity ratio is revealing, especially when it is tracked over time. In the example, the company has capitalized its operations with 43.4 percent debt, and the remainder with equity. If the percentage of debt were to increase over time—especially if profits did not also increase—that would be highly negative. Management may have

FIGURE 5.3 Debt/Equity Ratio (rounded to one decimal)

$$\frac{\text{Total Liabilities}}{\text{Net Worth} - \text{Intangible Assets}}$$

Example:
Total Liabilities	$32,063,764
Net Worth	$74,034,900
Intangible Assets	$ 235,000

$$\frac{\$32,063,764}{\$74,034,900 - \$235,000} = 43.4\%$$

worthwhile reasons to increase the debt capitalization of an operation, but only if that move improves profit margins as well.

🔑 KEY POINT

The debt/equity ratio can serve as a red flag. Watch out when the debt portion is rising over time, when profits remain at the same margin levels or, even worse, when profit margin begins to fall.

The ratios above should serve as the basic balance sheet ratios worth following, in addition to the even more common statement of income tests such as: sales, net profits, and net margin.

The Importance of Notes

The purpose of notes is to expand on what is shown in the financial statement, to provide additional information where necessary. The financial statement format does not always allow room for the full story. Accounting conventions tend to be highly conservative, numerous forms of information require notes for clarification. It is impossible for all of the significant information to be reported just with numbers, so explanatory notes form an essential element in the overall reporting of results. Ten examples:

1. *Market value is different than reported value.* When market value of assets is substantially different than book value, that may be discussed in a note, both for the asset and for its effect on net worth.
2. *Changes in accounting policy.* Changes in accounting policies will affect inventory, treatment of deferred income and expenses, and other important matters.
3. *Off-balance sheet liabilities.* Some liabilities do not show up on the balance sheet. For example, the corporation might be obligated to many years of payments under terms of an operating lease. However, that operating lease is not listed as a liability, which is one of the quirks of standard accounting.
4. *Contingent liabilities.* Companies may be aware of contingent liabilities and disclose them in a note. These are matters known to the company at the time the statement is prepared that are difficult to quantify, but that are important enough to disclose, such as pending lawsuits.
5. *Accounting explanations.* Some items simply require explanation. For example, a company will disclose its method for establishing and maintaining a reserve for bad debts.
6. *Nonfinancial disclosures.* Some matters not involving financial reporting directly will potentially have an affect on profit and loss. For example, the company might be aware of the threat of a labor strike that will involve a large portion of its workforce, interrupting production and therefore sales.
7. *Trading in company stock by officers and directors.* Executives and key employees of the corporation often are given stock or stock options. When an insider trades a significant number of shares, that may require an explanation. Likewise, the company itself might by buying up its own stock, a sign that the corporate management believes the current market price is a good deal. When companies buy their own stock, that stock does not have voting rights and no dividends are paid. Such repurchased stock is deducted in the shareholders' equity section of the balance sheet as an adjustment. It is called treasury stock.
8. *Disclosure of acquisitions and divestitures.* When the corporation acquires other companies or merges two operations into one, or when it divests itself of a subsidiary operation, that will be reported by way of a note.

9. *Adjustments from audits, credits, and carryovers.* Some accounting adjustments result from audits, either by an independent auditing firm or a government agency.

10. *Extraordinary items.* Corporations often experience adjustments in their financial picture due to outside influences or nonrecurring events. Examples include profit or loss from foreign exchange adjustments, catastrophic losses, losses resulting from labor problems, profits from investment in securities, and losses resulting from poor results in subsidiary operations.

Comparisons with Past Financial Reports

A financial statement is valuable as a single document only for testing of certain fundamentals. For example, if you accept the commonly held belief that current ratios should be 2-to-1 or better, it is easy to check that at a glance. However, for the more individualized forms of fundamental analysis, in which you are looking for trends and changes over time, you need to compare today's financial statements to those of the past.

Published statements include the latest two years of balance sheets and three years of other financial statements. Quarterly reports usually include comparisons only to results from the prior fiscal year's comparable quarters. This is adequate for a level of preliminary analysis; but when you own shares of stock in a company, your trend analysis should be ongoing, and should involve tests over as many years as you hold your stock. Two years represent only the two latest entries in a continuing trend.

Your task in the preliminary analysis of a financial statement is to quickly identify declining trends (when monitoring your portfolio) or favorable reversals (if you are thinking of buying the stock). These are not always easy to spot; however, some declining trends are obvious

★ KEY POINT

The comparison of two years is a good starting point, but a real trend requires more. Remember that the latest information is simply an entry in a longer history.

from a surface review. Some turnarounds do not become obvious until the opportunity has come and gone. In other words, there is always a degree of risk in interpreting trends. Declining sales, reduction in earnings per share, lowered dividend declaration or a missed dividend payment, and reduction in working capital (such as that expressed by the current ratio) are all examples of easy-to-spot declining trends. Dramatically improving sales over two or more periods, improvements in working capital, and improved net margin all are indicators of a potential turnaround in previous negative trends.

Be especially aware of the relative changes in working capital (current assets compared to current liabilities). This is where bigger problems often associated with expansion often appear first. As companies expand, good planning and management lead to the maintenance of minimum requirements in working capital. Growth occurring too quickly or without proper controls is reflected in declining working capital.

A second area to search for problems—especially when watching balance sheet ratios and trends over time—is in the relative makeup of capitalization. As dependence on debt increases, interest costs rise as well. That in itself is not a problem as long as profit margins are maintained and a higher dollar volume of profits is made possible. Such a situation demonstrates that management is using borrowed funds well while controlling net margin. Debt is appropriate when the dollar amount of profits increases enough to cover interest within the same margin, and it generates enough cash flow to repay the principal portion of borrowed money.

You can also look for declining trends on the statement of income. The most obvious will be net margin and earnings per share. Be cautious, however, in a year-to-year comparison of earnings per share. If additional common shares were issued during the year, then earnings per share cannot be tracked accurately. Likewise, if the company repurchased its own shares in large volume, retiring those shares to treasury stock, that distorts the comparison of earnings per share from one year to the next. Because treasury stock earns no dividends, that artificially raises the dividends for other stock. And finally, be aware of the dividends paid to preferred stockholders. Use the payout ratio rather than a more simplified earnings per share calculation to find any masked trends in this area.

One ratio to watch carefully tests dividend payments. Many investors like to watch the dividend rate over time. However, simply tracking the dividend rate may not tell the whole story. A more reveal-

FIGURE 5.4 Dividend Payout Ratio (rounded to one decimal)

$$\frac{\text{Dividends Paid on Common Stock}}{\text{Net Income} - \text{Dividends Paid on Preferred Stock}}$$

Example:

Dividends Paid on Common Stock	$ 300,000
Dividends Paid on Preferred Stock	$ 60,000
Net Income	$6,814,200

$$\frac{\$300,000}{\$6,814,200 - \$60,000} = 4.4\%$$

ing way to track dividends is through the dividend payout ratio (see Figure 5.4). This ratio also reports the percentage of dividends paid on common stock, but it adjusts for any dividends declared and paid on preferred stock. This provides you with an accurate tracking device for common stock dividends (which most stockholders receive), especially if the rate on preferred stock changes significantly on comparable profits. The formula involves dividing common stock dividends paid by adjusted net profits (net profits minus dividends paid on preferred stock); the result is expressed as a percentage.

In the example, the adjusted payout is 4.4 percent. A simple calculation of common stock dividends without excluding preferred dividends would not change this percentage. However, if the rate of payment on preferred stock were to change in the future, it would impact the common stock payout. Also if the corporation were to issue a large number of preferred stock shares and then declare and pay dividends, the payout would be affected. The payout ratio allows you to accurately track common stock dividends over time.

The dividend payout ratio reveals one important trend—how management pays dividends to shareholders after allowing for adjustments

✦ KEY POINT

The dividend payout ratio is useful in identifying the real payout trend, after adjusting for potentially changing management policies regarding preferred shareholders.

for preferred shareholders. This, in combination with careful monitoring of sales trends, forms the basis for a sound program of fundamental analysis.

While sales volume by itself should never be a decisive fundamental indicator, sales are important for purposes of comparison in ratio form. Thus, when sales decline from one period to another, it should raise questions. First, how have declining sales affected other important ratios, such as earnings per share and net margin? Why have sales declined? Is the decline a one-time event or part of a trend? If the company is ceding industry leadership to another corporation, do declining sales represent lost market share?

Equally as important as sales volume trends is the gross margin. This is the percentage that gross profit (sales less direct costs) represents when compared to sales.

Gross margin is an important fundamental test for the statement of income. The formula for gross margin is shown in Figure 5.5.

Gross margin should remain fairly constant, regardless of how sales rise or fall. Thus, in periods of rapid expansion, a deteriorating rate of

---

⚓ KEY POINT

Sales volume trends have always been popular indicators, although they do not tell the entire story. Use sales as a part of your broader statement of income analysis.

FIGURE 5.5 Gross Margin (rounded to one decimal)

$$\frac{\text{Gross Profit (Sales} - \text{Direct Costs)}}{\text{Sales}}$$

Example:
Sales	$86,445,000
Direct Costs	$51,005,000
Gross Profit	$35,440,000

$$\frac{\$35,440,000}{\$86,445,000} = 41.0\%$$

✦ KEY POINT

Gross margin often is ignored as a fundamental indicator. The ability or inability of management to maintain a consistent level of gross margin during times of rapid expansion is a valuable indicator.

gross margin is one indicator that profits will tend to erode. Management should carefully control its gross margin because direct costs should change directly in relationship to sales.

The most important of the balance sheet trends will be profitability—not only the amount of net profit, but the margin as well. The amount of net profit should be a reflection of sales volume. As volume increases, so should the amount of profit. However, it is possible to have higher dollar amount profit with lower net margin. This indicates that a company is producing more sales revenue, but lower rates of return, a negative trend. Some analysts look for ever-growing margins, which is not practical. However, a healthy growth period is characterized by stable net margins. That means that the dollar amount of profits rises with higher sales, but also that the percentage margin remains constant within an acceptable range. This is the case because it is unlikely that a corporation will be able to improve its net margin indefinitely.

An exception to this rule occurs when a company in one primary line of business acquires a subsidiary operation or merges with a corporation in a different product or service line, especially one with a significantly different level of net margin. As the two operations are combined, the mix of business will dictate what constitutes normal margins. In watching the profitability trend over time, be aware of the effect of mergers and acquisitions of dissimilar lines, and adjust the trend expectation accordingly.

✦ KEY POINT

Net margin should remain consistent within a reasonable range, and can be expected to change only when a corporation dramatically changes its mix of business, for example, through acquisitions.

Comparing a Company with Its Direct Competitors

Fundamental analysis, while generally thought of as applying to a single company, has equal importance in comparisons between corporations in the same industry. This is where the idea of normal margins, rates of growth, and all other statistical results can be put into perspective.

Comparisons within a single industry help to demonstrate the relative strength or weakness of the subject corporation to the norm and to other companies. It helps to identify not only which company is the leader today (in terms of competitive market share and profits, for example), but how that comparison changes over time. You should never assume that today's leaders will continue to lead in the future; company-to-company comparisons should play a significant role in your fundamental program—not only because comparisons can be made more valid in that manner, but also because emerging changes are the most likely form of fundamental analysis that will change a hold decision to a sell decision.

✦ KEY POINT

Today's industry leaders can change. Never assume that the current status within a particular industry will remain the same forever. Change is the only constant.

First, what is the subject company's position in the industry? You might want to invest in the clearly dominant company today and then monitor that position, deciding to hold as long as the company remains dominant. Or, you might want to try and use fundamental indicators to pick a likely heir-apparent to that position, the competitor that seems destined to take over the lead. The leading company's stock might be overvalued in comparison to another company in the industry, so that correctly forecasting the leader a decade from now could be more profitable than investing in the industry leader. That is more easily said than done, however; no one can know how the future will shape up, and it is very difficult to pick future industry leaders, even with the best fundamental analysis available.

As new leading industry competitors emerge, a series of events occurs that is worth watching. These events may include:

- Increased share of sales relative to other competitors
- Attraction of higher-quality management talent
- Innovation in new product and service technology
- Increasingly higher ratings for customer service
- Excellent reputation for relations between management and employees
- Rapid and profitable expansion of geographic markets
- Well-conceived expansion in lines of business; that is, diversification

Many other indicators will add to the equation. The absence of these and other attributes does not eliminate a company as a future leader; and the presence of these attributes does not ensure a change in leadership either.

A mistake made by many investors, especially in comparisons between companies within a single industry, is to assume that things never change; for example, that IBM will always lead the computer industry or Woolworth's will always lead in the retail sector. But change is not only inevitable; it is the nature of free enterprise. Change occurs as an attribute of competition itself. As competitors threaten to take over market share, others in the industry try harder, innovate more, take greater risks, and fight to not only hold on to what they have but to expand. New technology opens new markets, just as new generations of people create new consumer demands. The radio was replaced by the television, which today is being replaced rapidly by the Internet. It is difficult to imagine what future technological changes and consumer demands will drive markets, but by always being aware of the nature of change, you probably can spot industry changes as they begin to emerge.

No one should pretend that fundamental analysis—which is based on history—can accurately predict future trends and changes in competition and markets. However, the fundamentals are valuable precisely because of what they do provide: the first indications of change. It is not enough to identify change and then determine whether it is positive or negative. You also need to be able to understand why change occurs. For example, let's say you have invested in an industry that is losing profitability. These changes will show up in the fundamentals. By careful study of those trends, you may determine that it is time to sell. However, you also identify the cause of the change, which points to greater potential in a different industry. This gives you the clues you need to know where to invest your capital to maximize future growth.

KEY POINT

Fundamentals cannot predict the future, but the insightful analyst can use fundamentals to identify the first indications of emerging changes.

Become Your Own Expert

Perhaps the greatest challenge in making investment decisions is not the decision itself, but the question of choosing from among many, many indicators. The truly wise investor has strong beliefs about the validity of the limited number of indicators that are important to follow and use to make decisions.

The difficulty, then, is narrowing down your field of analysis. You would find decisions impossible if you were to consider and compare every possible form of fundamental analysis. At some point, you need to determine what ratios and formulas give you useful information. The rest may be interesting, but it must be rejected. You need to define and set priorities. Otherwise, you may find yourself spending all of your time analyzing. By the time you identify the right decision, opportunity has come and gone.

This is the problem for all investors, even those preferring technical indicators. Once an opportunity has been identified, a decision must be made. Markets move and change quickly, and successful investors must also be quick decision makers. A first step in this goal is to become informed about financial statements, comfortable with analyzing them, and proficient at narrowing the range of study so that you can quickly determine the current status of that company.

An informed view about financial statements comes about not from having accounting expertise. On the contrary, too much analytical and financial expertise may get in the way of investment sensibility. Accountants think about the numbers and spend a lot of energy with forecast about future numbers. Investors use the numbers to think about investment value and future investment value. These are vastly different points of view.

Financial statements, viewed by themselves, can marginalize the fundamental information you need and want. If part of an annual report, you should not ignore the accompanying materials. The three big sections of the annual report worth studying are:

1.   *Management's discussion of operations.* Here you can learn a lot about how management defines its role. How does it discuss the past, especially if the prior year was disappointing? What kinds of forecasts are made by management? Most important of all, were management's forecasts from past annual reports accurate?

2.   *Auditor's report.* Read the auditor's report thoroughly and carefully. Be sure you comprehend what is being said. Look for the fourth paragraph where any exceptions will be noted. Unless the auditor's report is clearly unqualified, you should investigate the significance of the qualification and determine how that affects the dependability of the published financial statements.

3.   *Notes.* Many observers believe the most important information is found in the notes. While fundamental analysts believe in the worth of the numbers, the notes might tell you whether or not the numbers tell the whole story. At the very least, the notes are good indicators about what special circumstances should be kept in mind when developing opinions based on those financial statements.

CHAPTER 6

Ratios—What They Are, How They Work

*C*ommunicating with numbers alone is difficult, tedious, and often ineffective. You need to gather information that is largely numerical, and express it in some form that makes sense—to you and to everyone else. Those with purely analytical minds will be comfortable with the numbers. However, the majority of investors—even those who follow the fundamentals—are not so analytical that the numbers are enough.

Even the most analytical of minds comprehends information more readily when it is expressed in a form that is easier to digest. A short, concise paragraph may be more revealing than a long column of numbers. A graph or chart tells you more in a glance than a page of dollar values and percentages. This is where the ratio is valuable. A ratio is an abbreviated form of expression that describes the relationship between two or more values. For example, if one number is twice as large as another, the ratio of the two numbers is 2-to-1.

A ratio may be the result of a simple division of one value by another, or it may be a calculation of a more complex formula. In either event,

➤ *KEY POINT*

A number reflects value; a ratio reflects the relationship between two or more values.

a value derived from the comparison of two other values serves as a useful device for compiling fundamental information, and for enabling yourself to more easily understand the meaning of that information.

Example: This year, sales were $505,916,003 and net profits were $49,492,095. Last year, sales were $425,885,623 and net profit was $44,052,384.

In the above example using numbers alone, it is difficult to comprehend exactly how this year's results compare to last year's. While the current sales and profit numbers are higher, are they better? This depends, of course, on the standard for comparison that you want to use. If that standard is net margin, then the results are not positive. Using ratios like net margin (net profits expressed as a percentage of sales), a year-to-year comparison is much easier.

This year, net margin was 9.8 percent, compared with 10.3 percent last year. Not only is stating the comparison as net margin shorter, it is more precise. It communicates not just the numbers, but the significance of those numbers. You can quickly learn that net margin is down this year. It is not necessary to go through a calculation because the ratio is the result of a calculation that has been done already.

Fundamentals should not be used for short-term decision making, but for management of a long-term portfolio. Indicators are developed from the compilation of consistently developed information. That does not require that you ensure its exact accuracy; it is more important that the information be generally reliable and applied consistently in all cases. The following example will clarify this point.

Example: You realize that the current ratio, as important a test as it is, cannot be considered completely accurate. Because current asset and liability account balances change from time to time, the year-end totals might not be entirely representative. It would be more accurate to perform a current ratio using a 12-month average that is recalculated every month.

While the point is a valid one, do you really want to compile running monthly totals for current assets and current liabilities, and compute a running average each month? It would provide more accuracy, but would it make a significant difference? In this book, a basic premise is that simplified, straightforward information is good enough in most cases, as long as the same approach is used in each and every case.

➤ KEY POINT

Fundamental analysis does not need to be exact to be valuable. As long as you get important information that is reliable and consistent, you do not need absolute accuracy.

Every ratio you use should provide you with certain basic things, including:

- *Validity.* A ratio must provide you with meaningful information.
- *Value.* A ratio also should provide you with information that indicates the latest entry in a trend that you need to follow in order to manage your portfolio.
- *Practicality.* If you are to succeed in developing a fundamental program, it has to be simple enough so that you can maintain it.

Forms of Ratios

A ratio is any value resulting from the comparison between two or more related values. In this book, the term ratio is applied liberally to many formulas and calculations that, strictly speaking, are not ratios. However, for the purpose of maintaining a focus on the desired result, all of these processes are called ratios. Any time the result is expressed in an abbreviated form it will be called a ratio.

There are four methods for expressing ratios. They are:

1. *Dollar amount.* An abbreviated expression in the form of dollar value is one popular method for expressing ratio values. It is applicable only when dealing with financial information in comparison with some other value, and when the result makes sense as a dollar value. For example, earnings per share is always expressed as a dollar value. The overall earnings (net profit) represents the total earnings for the entire corporation. When that is divided by the number of outstanding shares of common stock, the result is per-share earnings, or a dollar amount.

2. *Percentage.* The use of percentages to express financial value is one of the most popular and widely used methods of com-

municating. Financial statements often contain percentage expressions, especially on the statement of income. One form of expression even provides for the exclusive use of percentages in place of dollar amounts. Thus, the abbreviated form of the statement of income would appear as:

Total sales	100.00%
Cost of sales	61.32
Gross profit	38.68%
Expenses	27.94
Net profit	10.74%

Percentages are used in a variety of other ratios, notably those comparing one dollar amount to another (profit to sales, bonds to total capitalization, and so forth).

3. *Value* x *to value* y. The shorthand version of the ratio is used for ratios such as the current ratio, where one group of dollar amounts is compared to another. The minimum standard normally requires a current ratio of 2-to-1, also expressed as 2/1. The x to y format breaks down dollar values in a way that is readily comprehended at a glance and that makes it easy to compare results from year to year.

4. *The number of times or occurrences.* Many ratios involve studying the number of times an event occurs. For example, when a ratio demonstrates the number of times inventory is turned over (sold and replaced), the result is expressed as the number of times that happens. So when you see a turnover of 7 versus previous turnover rates of 4 or 5, that is a significant slowdown. (More on turnover below.)

If you develop a ratio on your own, you should select the expression that most aptly fits with the information you are studying. If you prefer one method over another and you believe it provides you with better insight about what the numbers reveal, you should change even a standard method to suit your own needs.

Balance Sheet and Earnings Ratios

The balance sheet reports the values of assets, liabilities, and net worth as of the closing date of a reporting period (the end of the fiscal year, for example). Some important key ratios involving balance sheet accounts were explained in previous chapters, including the current ratio, quick assets ratio, debt/equity ratio, and dividend payout ratio.

Inventory Turnover

Calculate inventory turnover by dividing the cost of sales by inventory at cost. This ratio shows how well management has controlled inventory levels during the year. Ideally, higher turnover is desirable because it shows that inventory levels are not excessive. However, an extremely high turnover also might indicate that inadequate levels of inventory are maintained resulting in back orders and increased cost of sales. A trend developed to study turnover levels will show seasonal variation and enable you to track changes occurring in periods of growth or slowdown.

The calculation for inventory turnover is shown in Figure 6.1.

Some analysts prefer to use sales in place of cost of sales in the turnover calculation. This is less accurate because inventory levels are reported at cost, whereas sales are marked up. So a shift in the product lines will affect sales-based turnover and distort the ratio. For example, if one line of business is marked up 50 percent and another 100 percent, a substantial shift from one line to another in the mix of overall sales will change the turnover calculation, while inventory levels might be stable in actual practice.

FIGURE 6.1   Inventory Turnover (rounded to one decimal)

$$\frac{\text{Cost of Sales}}{\text{Inventory at Cost}}$$

Example:
Cost of Sales $51,005,000
Inventory at Cost $11,943,800

$$\frac{\$51,005,000}{\$11,943,800} = 4.3 \text{ Times}$$

⚡ *KEY POINT*

Calculation of inventory turnover should use cost of sales, not sales. Because sales are marked up, they cannot be reliably compared to inventory at cost.

Working Capital Turnover

The current ratio, which was discussed in an earlier chapter, provides you with a general idea of the relative strength of working capital. It shows how well management keeps a balance between assets and liabilities, so that cash is available now (and will be in the immediate future) to fund operations—essential to keeping a business healthy.

One problem with the current ratio is that it does not always present a clear picture. For example, overly high cash balances, too-slow collection of receivables, and excessively high inventory levels might all be financed with long-term debt, a serious problem that does not show up in the current ratio. In such a case, the severity of the problem might become evident only when the company's stability is already compromised. To avoid this problem, compare working capital to sales.

⚡ *KEY POINT*

Although current ratio is a popular and widely used ratio, it may be unreliable for spotting emerging problems in control of current asset accounts.

The calculation of working capital turnover shows how current assets and current liabilities are related to the generation of sales. This ratio assumes that working capital (the difference between current assets and current liabilities) is related directly to the production of sales volume. Because working capital is essential to the continuation of operations, there is a true relationship. In fact, calculating working capital turnover exposes artificial current ratio results. If a

FIGURE 6.2 Working Capital Turnover (rounded to one decimal)

$$\frac{Sales}{Current\ Assets - Current\ Liabilities}$$

Example:
Sales	$86,445,000
Current Assets	$23,410,000
Current Liabilities	$10,049,400

$$\frac{\$86,445,000}{\$23,410,000 - \$10,049,400} = 6.5\ Times$$

2-to-1 current ratio does not adequately show excessively high account balance levels in the current asset categories, such a problem will be seen in declining turnover rates in working capital. A problem invisible in current ratio analysis may be exposed through working capital turnover trends.

The calculation of working capital turnover is shown in Figure 6.2.

The number of times that working capital is used and replaced is an average, not an actual calculation of liquidated accounts. In practice, current assets and liabilities are not totally used and replaced; their relative size does change over time, however.

With this ratio, you face the same problem as that of inventory in the study of inventory turnover: Are ending balances of assets and liabilities adequate for use in this ratio? Considering that sales reflect activity over a period of time—for example, one year—and asset and liability balances reflect only the ending balances, the ratio might not accurately reflect turnover if those balances have changed.

It is probably more accurate to use averages in current accounts for the applicable period, rather than ending balances only. For example, if significant shifts have occurred from the beginning of the year to the end of the year, then the turnover analysis should reflect the significance of that change.

Finding the average for current assets and liabilities is a simple matter. If you have a published statement of cash flow, the change in current accounts will be shown on the statement itself. If you only have a balance sheet available, compare current to prior year balances. Add the two values for current assets together and divide by two; repeat the averaging process for current liabilities.

Diluted Earnings Per Share

The primary earnings per share (basic EPS) test is not always the most accurate way to measure. Stock options, if on the books in considerable numbers, will drastically affect the dilution of earnings, and also should be considered when going through the calculation. (Dilution is the reduction in book value per share of stock that occurs when new shares are sold or options exercised.)

To ensure that comparisons are accurate, you need to be aware of the effects of dilution and how it might affect the earnings per share calculation. To understand how dilution works, review the basic attributes of convertible securities. The process of conversion involves exchanging one form of investment for another. This would occur at a point that shares of common stock are equal to or surpass the value of the currently owned security. When the two securities are of equal value, they are at parity.

The first form of convertible security includes some forms of preferred stock. This is a class of stock generally less risky than common stock because shareholders have priority for payment of dividends and for liquidation in cases of bankruptcy. Preferred shareholders do not have voting rights, as common shareholders do. Some forms of preferred stock may be classified as convertible preferred stock. This means the shareholders may exercise the right to convert preferred stock to common stock by a specified deadline and/or at a predetermined price per share. This option to convert would make sense if and when the market price of a share of common stock reached or exceeded parity.

The second form of convertible security is the convertible bond. This feature often is added to bonds as a means for marketing them to investors. The right to convert to common stock would become attractive if the market value of stock exceeded that level, or if the interest rate being earned on the bond turned out to be low compared to prevailing market rates.

With the types of convertible securities in mind, the concept of dilution—and the effect it might have on the calculation of earnings per share—is more easily appreciated. When a company carries convertible preferred stock or bonds on its books, that does not mean that conversion will occur. Of course, if the stock's market price were to reach and/or exceed parity, then conversion is virtually certain. If you are comparing the earnings of such a company with those of another company that does not carry any convertible securities, then the comparison is not really the same. The effects of dilution in the event of conversion have to be taken into account. Bonds and preferred stock converted to common stock reduce the earnings per share.

FIGURE 6.3   Diluted Earnings Per Share

$$\frac{\text{Net Profit} + \text{Conversion Value}}{\text{Outstanding Shares after Conversion}}$$

Example:
Net Profit	$6,814,200
Conversion Value	$ 400,000
Outstanding Shares after Conversion	2,500,000

$$\frac{\$6,814,200 + \$400,000}{2,500,000} = \$2.89$$

Thus, a new calculation is required to account for the contingent effect of conversion. If conversion were to occur, earnings per share would be diluted; the greater the dollar amount of convertible securities and the higher the number of common shares involved, the greater the effect of dilution will be. The calculation of diluted earnings per share involves two modifications to the more common primary earnings per share. First, the net profit is increased by the conversion value of all convertible preferred stock and convertible bonds. Second, the outstanding shares of common stock are increased to reflect the new number of such shares that would exist after conversion.

The formula for diluted earnings per share is shown in Figure 6.3.

The important point to remember about using diluted versus basic earnings per share is that so doing makes the comparison accurate and consistent when comparing earnings per share for two or more corporations when not all of them offer convertible securities. If you are watching a trend in one company only, or if you are comparing two corporate earnings per share where neither have convertible securities, then dilution is not an issue.

✦ KEY POINT

Tracking earnings per share in two dissimilar companies will not be accurate if convertible securities are on the books in either of the companies. Calculate diluted earnings per share to solve this problem.

Capitalization Ratios

You also will need to observe a company's policies concerning capitalization. In previous chapters, you saw how the debt/equity ratio shows how well a company mixes debt and equity.

Capitalization is made up of several sources, some from equity (capital stock and retained earnings) and some from debt (long-term notes, contracts, and bonds). For many publicly listed corporations, a significant portion of capitalization consists of bonds. These are debt instruments sold to the general public and traded on the exchange, like stocks. Below is a quick review of some of the features of bonds.

★ KEY POINT

Tracking the mix of capitalization is one valuable way to spot emerging trends and possible trouble spots.

Bonds are contractual obligations of the company. There are many forms and various types of security, including unsecured bonds, called debentures. The bond agreement states the interest rate that will be paid throughout the life of the bond and the date on which the bond will be repaid. Investors buy bonds from corporations as well as from government entities (both federal and state subdivisions of them) and from local municipalities. Some forms of bonds offer tax advantages, while others are designed to pay a higher interest rate.

Because the interest rate is established in advance and does not change, bonds may become more or less desirable as investments over time. Bonds can be traded publicly, so a bond whose interest rate is high in relation to current rates will demand a higher market price than the actual par value of the bond. When this occurs, the bond trades at a premium. For example, a bond traded at 100 is trading at par. If a bond whose par value is $1,000 is traded at a premium of 104, its market value is $1,040. The safety rating of the issuer also affects market value.

When the set interest rate is below current prevailing rates, the bond becomes less attractive and its market value falls. When this occurs, the bond trades at a discount. If a bond whose par value is $1,000 is traded at a discount of 94, its market value is $940.

This very brief overview is provided for the purpose of explaining that bonds play an important role in publicly traded corporate capitalization. A bond is carried as a liability because the corporation must repay bondholders at a specified date in the future, regardless of whether there are profits to pay dividends. However, the greater the degree of capitalization represented by bonds, the greater the interest payment obligation is from year to year. If a corporation comes to rely on bond capitalization more and more each year, while profits do not increase to justify interest expense, the entire profitability structure may begin to fail.

★ KEY POINT

The greater the dollar amount of bonds on the books, the greater the obligation to pay interest. That erodes future profits for funding operations and for paying dividends to stockholders.

For the common stock investor, this has serious ramifications. Profits maintain a stock's market price, and earnings are the primary indicator over the long term. Year-to-year growth has to consist of a series of earnings levels meeting an acceptable standard. However, if the corporation depends too heavily on long-term debt capitalization, then profits begin to be transferred over time away from shareholders to bondholders. Eventually, dividends are replaced by interest payments to bondholders. When that occurs, market value suffers.

For this reason, you need to include in your fundamental analysis an ongoing study of total capitalization. You need to watch how the relationship between equity and debt changes over time. The three major components to capitalization are (1) bonds, (2) preferred stock, and (3) common stock. (Common stock's segment of capitalization should include retained earnings.) You should test the three components continuously through ratio analysis.

Bond Ratio

To compute bond ratio, divide the dollar amount of bonds by the dollar amount of total capitalization. This ratio tells you how much of total

FIGURE 6.4 Bond Ratio (rounded to one decimal)

$$\frac{\text{Bonds}}{\text{Total Capitalization}}$$

Example:
  Bonds $15,000,000
  Total Capitalization $89,034,900

$$\frac{\$15,000,000}{\$89,034,900} \;=\; 16.8\%$$

capitalization is composed of debt, consisting of outstanding bonds. The formula for the bond ratio is shown in Figure 6.4.

Preferred Stock Ratio

To compute preferred stock ratio, divide the dollar amount of preferred stock by the dollar amount of total capitalization. This ratio shows you what portion of total capitalization is represented by preferred stock and, by tracking from year to year, whether that relationship is changing.

The formula for the preferred stock ratio is shown in Figure 6.5.

FIGURE 6.5 Preferred Stock Ratio (rounded to one decimal)

$$\frac{\text{Preferred Stock}}{\text{Total Capitalization}}$$

Example:
  Preferred Stock $ 1,200,000
  Total Capitalization $89,034,900

$$\frac{\$1,200,000}{\$89,034,900} \;=\; 1.4\%$$

Common Stock Ratio

To compute common stock ratio, add together the dollar values of common stock and retained earnings, then divide by total capitalization. This shows the portion of total capitalization held by common shareholders.

The formula for the common stock ratio is shown in Figure 6.6.

FIGURE 6.6 Common Stock Ratio (rounded to one decimal)

$$\frac{\text{Common Stock + Retained Earnings}}{\text{Total Capitalization}}$$

Example:

Common Stock	$11,450,960
Retained Earnings	$61,383,940
Total Capitalization	$89,034,900

$$\frac{\$11,450,960 + \$61,383,940}{\$89,034,900} = 81.8\%$$

The total of ratios for the three tests above should equal 100 percent. The purpose of these ratios is not merely to calculate the relative degree of capitalization represented by each group; it is to track that relationship over time. You will want to know if the relative influence of debt is increasing with time, especially if profits are not exceeding the cost of debt service, which is represented by interest expense.

🔑 KEY POINT

The combination of bond, preferred stock, and common stock ratios should equal 100 percent, representing total capitalization.

Interest Coverage

One final capitalization ratio worth remembering is interest coverage. This ratio shows how many multiples of bond interest are available from operating profit. In other words, it shows the relative "coverage," or multiples, of operating profit compared to the cost of borrowing capital through bonds.

Interest coverage enables you to spot trends over time, especially if increasing bond interest obligations are demanding ever-increasing levels of net profits.

To compute, divide operating profit (profit before interest and taxes) by the dollar amount of bond interest paid during the past year. The result is expressed as the number of times, an indicator of coverage from profits to pay for bond interest. The value in this ratio is what it demonstrates over time, especially when used in combination with other important ratio tests. Your concern about debt capitalization should be to determine whether management is keeping debt capital in perspective, given a company's growth potential and current profitability. If the coverage rate, demonstrated by this ratio, begins to fall from one period to another, that is a sign that management is allowing debt capitalization to edge too high.

The formula for computing interest coverage is shown in Figure 6.7.

FIGURE 6.7 Interest Coverage (rounded to one decimal)

$$\frac{\text{Net Profit before Interest and Taxes}}{\text{Bond Interest}}$$

Example:

Net Profit	$6,814,200
Interest Expense	1,218,400
Taxes	1,916,100
Net Profit before Interest and Taxes	$9,948,700
Bond Interest	$1,140,000

$$\frac{\$9,948,700}{\$1,140,000} = 8.7 \text{ Times}$$

Profitability Ratios Based on Original Investment

The standard test of profitability involves net margin (net income compared to sales) or earnings per share (net profit expressed on a per-share basis). Another way to look at the idea of profitability is to consider how the shareholders' investment grows over time. With this in mind, the following section presents another category of ratios: profitability on the basis of the original investment.

Return on Equity

In most forms of investment, the standard calculation involves a comparison between the income from the investment and the amount actually invested. In other words, you invest $1,000 in the purchase of stock and you receive $1,100—a margin of 10 percent. Or you buy a house for $150,000 and later sell it for $180,000, for a margin of 20 percent.

Only when it comes to corporate financial statements is this general rule not followed. The standard concept of margin and return is based on the business activity rather than on investment value. However, there are two levels of analysis going on at the same time. As a fundamental analyst, you need to keep these two levels separate in your mind.

First is the standard evaluation that occurs in corporations' accounting departments. Business success is invariably measured in terms of sales. How much profit was generated? How did that compare to last year? Why wasn't it more? Dollars are the scorekeeping medium in business. And because the study and reporting of financial results is universal and standardized, this has also become the basis for most fundamental analysis—appropriately so.

The second, more subtle, evaluation is return on your personal investment. Why is this more subtle? First of all, in the preoccupation with fundamental analysis based on performance measured against sales volume, and financial strength judged by assets, it is easy to overlook the all-important bottom line for you, the investor. Ultimately, it is the return on your capital, not the corporation's capital, that is important to you. What good does it do you if the corporation's profits set new records if you still show a loss when you sell your stock?

The formula for calculating year-to-year overall return on investment is different if you continue to hold a stock than it would be if you had sold. After a sale, the calculation involves a comparison between the purchase price and the sale price. In the most simplistic form, the difference is a profit (selling price is higher than the purchase price) or a loss (selling price is lower than the purchase price). In more complex forms of analysis, you might add in dividend receipts to arrive at total return. If you also consider the length the investment was held, you would also divide total return by the number of years to arrive at annualized return. This is an important distinction to make from total return.

Example: You have two separate investments, one which you purchased ten years ago and one which you purchased only one year ago. You sold both investments this year. The older of the two yielded 58 percent in total return; the newer investment yielded a total return of 8 percent.

This example demonstrates the importance of annualizing total return. It helps to make your comparisons truly comparative. Considering that you had the one investment for ten years, the average annualized margin was 5.8 percent. In comparison, the newer investment yielded 8 percent, which was higher on the annual basis.

Annualized return is also helpful in calculating comparative returns on investments held for less than one full year.

Example: You sold two stocks this year. Both yielded 11 percent in total return. The first was held for 13 months, while the second was held for only 8 months.

To compute annualized return for partial years, first divide the total return by the number of months held, and then multiply by 12 (months). The result is the equivalent annual margin.

Example A:
11 percent total return, 13 months:

$$\frac{11}{13} = .846$$

.846 x 12 (months) = 10.15% annualized return

Example B:
11 percent total return, 8 months:

$$\frac{8}{13} = .615$$

.615 x 12 (months) = 7.38% annualized return

As you can see, annualizing returns for investments held over different periods can clarify your profit picture. One of the most important rules for fundamental analysts is to ensure that the conclusions they draw are always based on truly comparative information.

The analysis of profits on stocks already sold is relatively easy, because you know the dollar amounts involved as well as the holding period. However, you may also want to calculate the return-to-date on investments you currently hold, as a means to determine whether the decision to hold the investment makes sense. If the rate of return on your investment is below your expectation level, that alone might be enough to trigger a sell decision. Thus, it is always wise to calculate your total annualized return based on the question: What would the outcome be if I sold today?

Another twist on this form of analysis is to ask yourself what shareholders are earning as a return on their investment in the company. This is not the same as the analysis of your investment in the stock, meaning comparing purchase price to sales price of the stock. A study of shareholders' return has to compare net profits from operations, to average net worth for the latest year. The ratio for return on equity is shown in Figure 6.8.

FIGURE 6.8   Return on Equity (rounded to one decimal)

$$\frac{\text{Net Income}}{\text{Average Net Worth}}$$

Example:

Net Income	$ 6,814,200
Net Worth, End of Year	$74,034,900
Net Worth, Beginning of Year	$67,220,700
Average Net Worth	$70,627,800

$$\frac{\$6,814,200}{\$70,627,800} = 9.6\%$$

This ratio shows not the volatility of the market price of the stock, but how the investment in capital stock—becoming a shareholder in the corporation—performed on the basis of income generated during the year. In truth, return by way of net income is only the current income portion of the investment. In the longer-term sense, it is the market value of stock that will determine return on equity. This ratio enables you to develop a way to monitor operational performance by the corporation based not so much on sales growth, but on the relationship between net income and equity capital.

🦅 KEY POINT

Ultimately, return on equity will mean much more to you as an investor than the corporate measurement of net margin on sales.

Average net worth is important to calculate, because using only the year-end figure ignores current additions to retained earnings from net income, as well as any new stock issued during the year. To compute, add the total net worth at the beginning of the year to total net worth at the end of the year and divide the total by two.

Growth Ratios

Most analysts agree that growth is a good thing, because it is necessary to maintain a competitive edge, to expand profits and lines of business, and to maintain control over expenses so that profits do not erode over time. However, growth should take place in a controlled manner, and under the careful guidance of management. Overly rapid growth brings numerous problems with it.

⚡ *KEY POINT*

Growth, although a positive and necessary process, is dangerous to the financial health of the corporation unless it is planned and controlled. One of the more important fundamental tests you can perform is one that measures not just growth, but management's ability—and willingness—to control the rate of growth.

For each corporations in which you invest, you need to know the (1) growth in sales and (2) growth in earnings per share. These ratios are useful not only for watching the rate of growth and ensuring that it continues, but also for determining that growth is not occurring too quickly.

Growth in Sales

You probably already recognize that the study of sales volume, by itself, is not a reliable indicator. Volume is only part of the expansion and profitability equation. However, in terms of measuring the rate of growth, comparisons of increases in sales levels from year to year are very instructive. This ratio helps you to identify consistency in the rate of growth, and also to identify sudden changes in that rate.

The formula for growth in sales is shown in Figure 6.9.

This formula begins with the identification of a base year, the starting point to which all future years will be compared. In developing

FIGURE 6.9 Growth in Sales (rounded to one decimal)

$$\frac{\text{Sales in Latest Year}}{\text{Sales in Base Year}}$$

Example:
    Sales in Latest Year $86,445,000
    Sales in Base Year $68,401,700

$$\frac{\$86,445,000}{\$68,401,700} \ = \ 26.4\%$$

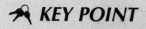 **KEY POINT**

Testing and tracking sales by itself is not adequate fundamental analysis. However, carefully watching sales as an indicator of growth pattern provides you with valuable fundamental information about management.

trends, the longer the period, the better. If you have the information available, you may decide to pick a far past base year. However, you might want to pick a base year that makes sense based on the history of the corporation. For example, the current growth in the stock might be based on a merger 12 years ago. The year of the merger or the first full year of combined operations would make a sensible base year.

As an alternative, you can identify the base year as the year you purchased stock in the company. In that way, you tie in the portfolio analysis to your own investment experience.

Growth in Earnings Per Share

A second ratio for identifying growth involves comparisons of earnings per share. In a growth stock, you should reasonably expect that the earnings per share would increase over time, assuming that profitability is reflected in market perceptions of value. And if that perception does not respond to the fundamental history, that could be an indication of some other problem. For example, the industry itself

FIGURE 6.10 Growth in Earnings Per Share (rounded to one decimal)

$$\frac{\text{Earnings Per Share in Latest Year}}{\text{Earnings Per Share in Base Year}}$$

Example:
  Earnings Per Share in Latest Year $3.75
  Earnings Per Share in Base Year $3.18

$$\frac{\$3.75}{\$3.18} = 17.9\%$$

➤ KEY POINT

Just as earnings per share is an important measurement of growth, the rate of change from year to year demonstrates how well one company is able to continue profitable growth from year to year. A truly professional management team will be able not only to create profits, but to continue a satisfactory rate of growth over many years.

might be out of favor with the investing public, or your company might be suffering from negative news of a direct competitor.

The ratio for growth in earnings per share is shown in Figure 6.10.

Like the growth in sales ratio, this ratio compares the latest year's figures to those in a base year. You should select the base year on the same reasoning as that used for growth in sales. If you use both of these ratios, use the same base year. The selection should also make sense as a base for each of the ratios involved. A well chosen base year is essential in ensuring that the results of the growth tests are reliable.

Developing a Ratio-Based Program

The combination of various ratios provides useful information. Too many people approach the question of analysis by simply following one or two ratios they consider important—and then study those in isolation. This is not an effective way to measure a company's financial performance. Below are a few typical combinations of ratios that may work well together to provide an overview of financial results. They are paired together with the purpose of enabling you to judge various factors at the same time.

Basic approach. This combination includes the ratios that should be in your program without exception. These ratios are the current ratio, the debt/equity ratio, and the dividend payout ratio. You do not want to limit your review to just these ratios, but if you look at nothing else, these ratios provide you with the bare minimum of information and a quick glance at a financial statement, the foundation for your analysis program.

Working capital approach.   This method combines the current ratio (and perhaps the quick assets ratio) with working capital turnover and inventory turnover. This approach is especially useful when companies are in significant growth periods—often recognized by large jumps in sales volume. By using working capital tests as a method for monitoring the company, you can anticipate how well operations will be controlled in future, larger volume periods.

Capitalization approach.   You also may be concerned when corporations appear to depend heavily on debt capitalization. If long-term liabilities and bonds represent too large a portion of capital, it makes sense to combine the bond ratio, preferred stock ratio, and common stock ratio, as well as watching carefully the trends in diluted earnings per share.

When are bonds too much of total capitalization? One important test is to compare earnings per share and net profit margin at various funding levels. As long as the corporation is able to maintain or improve profits and profit margins with higher debt, there is no problem. The danger occurs when profits and profit margins begin to erode as shareholders' returns are replaced with interest payments to bondholders. Include interest coverage in this approach to watch out for deteriorating relationships between net profit and interest being paid on bonds. This approach monitors the use of profits and capital trends.

Margin approach.   Earlier in this chapter, you saw how return on equity is a valuable ratio. It demonstrates how well shareholders fare on their investment performance, rather than comparing profit margins from one year to the next. Under the margin approach, you combine analysis of margins in various forms: return on equity, net margin, and earnings per share. This approach is useful when done in combination with price-earnings (PE) ratio, because it enables you to track financial results (fundamentals) with market price performance—the perception of fundamental value in the market as a whole. In a perfect world, the margin approach should anticipate the PE ratio in a predictable manner. In the real world of the auction marketplace, you will find that perceptions (market price and PE ratio) anticipate future margin. It is upside down. As a result, the perception may be right or wrong, and only time will tell. However, the margin approach provides you with an excellent method to determine the relationship between fundamentals and market price of the stock.

Growth approach. Tracking growth in sales is valuable because it uses a base year and calculates annual percentage increases. Likewise, tracking the annual changes in earnings per share from a base year clarifies the analysis and smoothes out exceptional years. This is an approach few investors take, because few people understand the importance of creating a base. It is from that base that growth is accurately measured.

The more popular way of measuring growth is from year to year. This is misleading and inaccurate. Each year, by itself, will not be representative of a base or of any relative and meaningful comparison. If you want to track growth and recognize reliable trends, you need to have a base year for virtually all of the fundamental analysis you perform.

For some ratios, like the current ratio, the base is the minimum standard of 2-to-1 or better. But for most other types of ratios, a base exists in time (e.g., a base year), and all future analysis grows from that base. So if the base is inaccurate or unreliable, the trend analysis itself will be flawed. Choosing the right base is critically important.

CHAPTER 7

Trends—
Your Secret Weapon

*A*fter developing a program for the identification and computation of ratios, you next will need to determine how to gather the ratios together and express them. Ratios serve a valuable function by escaping from the confusion in columns of values, because ratios reduce those values to abbreviated forms of expression. To gain full value from ratios you must compile them so that the trend that is uncovered by the ratios can be observed over time.

Trends may be positive or negative. But rarely does the indicated direction of a trend remain unchanged forever. Over time, trends tend to flatten out in some manner. For example, sales may increase from year to year, but the rate of increase tends to slow down over time. As a result, sales will appear to plateau. Most progressive trends—those following dollar amounts and increases from one year to the next—tend to experience this flattening out. This is why it is helpful with many trends to establish a base year, and measure the trend from there. As one directional trend is established and begins to plateau, you may then begin a program of new analysis—identifying a new base year and starting fresh.

The occasional replacement of one series of fundamental tests with a new set—even if only establishing a new base year—helps you to keep the fundamental analysis program current and relevant. Because trends flatten, longer periods of time tend to provide less and less information. You cannot depend entirely on more information and always assume that it is also better information.

🔑 *KEY POINT*

Be flexible. Replace your fundamental tests with other tests if that is what it takes to ensure reliable information.

Starting anew every few years helps overcome one of the consequences of the law of large numbers. This concept in probability and logic states that if you study a large enough sample of a population, you can predict outcomes with a high degree of accuracy. For example, we know that tossing a coin has a 50 percent chance of coming up heads or tails. If you apply only two tests, your results may not be 50 percent every time, but if you perform enough tests, you certainly will see results that grow increasingly close to 50 percent as the number of tests rises.

The downside of the law of large numbers is the predictability itself. As you study trends of a financial nature, it tells you very little if all of your tests plateau out, and you are basing conclusions on too large a population. As a general rule, you should replace a program and start from a zero base every few years, just to avoid the trap of the law of large numbers.

🔑 *KEY POINT*

The law of large numbers helps statisticians make accurate predictions; the same law can cloud information if it is applied in the wrong manner.

The averaging of trends helps to show overall direction over a period of a few months or years. However, using too long a period distorts the outcome.

Applying Ratios

What does a trend reveal? This is the essential question that you will ask constantly as your program evolves. If you do not know, or if a trend reveals nothing conclusively, then it has no real value. The valuable trend reveals some information you need to answer four basic questions:

1. Does this stock continue to offer the growth potential I sought when I first bought it?
2. Have the basic indicators changed, so that I now should sell?
3. Are the indicators continuing to operate within the acceptable range, so that I should continue to hold?
4. If I am thinking about buying a stock, what does the trend tell me in terms of whether that decision makes sense?

These basic questions (and their answers) ultimately determine all of your actions as an investor. You seek some source of consistently reliable information in order to make the decisions and to take action or to opt for inaction.

In the application of ratios as continuing entries in an ongoing trend, you need to identify a sensible base year or date. Why? Trends are comparative, and a starting point is essential. In the case of the current ratio, your base is a widely accepted standard: 2-to-1. For most other forms of ratio, the base should be a period that identifies your understanding of the stock—the date you purchased shares makes sense, for example. If the company had a major acquisition or merger within the past three to five years, the beginning date of that action may also serve as a base point for many forms of fundamental analysis. Otherwise, a date—such as the ending date of the latest fiscal year—can serve as your base point.

🔑 KEY POINT

Establishing a relevant base point is essential. With the wrong base point, your analysis will not give you the information you need to make good decisions.

In identifying trends from the base point on out, you will want to have some method for judging results graphically. Seeing the result is always more revealing than simply reading it. Just as ratios are easier to comprehend than columns of dollar values, a graphic representation of a trend makes more sense than a mere list of outcomes. (It's the "a picture is worth a thousand words" syndrome.)

A graph helps you to turn ratios into visual aids, showing the direction of movement over time in the collection of data. Graphs are not merely illustrations of what is occurring; it is entirely likely that the graph is the only method by which you can actually see what the trend means. That is because you need the graph to add perspective to the numerical values. While the ratio is a preferred method of expression over columns of numbers—because the ratio expresses the significance rather than the mere dollar amount—it is still a series of numbers. Only when those numbers are expressed in a visual manner can you truly appreciate the importance, degree, and change in an ongoing trend.

Some rules for preparing graphs follow.

For multiple graphs, always use the same scale.   Scaling is all-important in making your graph. First of all, the scale has to be practical so that your graph fits in a manageable amount of space. Second, the scale should remain constant when you will be using two or more comparable graphs. That is, if one inch equals a million dollars in one graph, that same scale should prevail in correlated graphs.

✦ KEY POINT

Pay close attention to the scaling of your graph. Proper scaling ensures reliable information, whereas improper scaling distorts information and the relationships among supposedly similar graphs.

Use the right base line.   Too many graphs misrepresent the numerical information because they do not show the relationships between two values. For example, if your graph includes dollar values, it is accurate to have the base line at zero; in too many instances, the range of a graph includes only enough space to show the data. Thus, an increase from $200,000 to $250,000 looks different than it would on a true scale.

This idea is illustrated in Figure 7.1. Note that the first graph shows a range from $190,000 through $260,000 so that the change over time appears to span the entire vertical range of the graph—a dramatic increase, visually. However, the second example shows the entire dollar amount range from zero to $300,000, so that the actual change is put into a more realistic perspective.

Such a dramatic change in information imparted as that shown in the figure is not unusual. If you begin to look critically at graphs as they are published in magazines and textbooks, you will discover that many rudimentary scaling problems distort the message entirely. Rather than clarifying a point, the visual aid distorts it.

⚔ KEY POINT

When it comes to your program of fundamental analysis, you want to ensure that at the very least, you do not deceive yourself.

Keep it simple. The suggestion that you develop your own system of graphic trend analysis does not mean that you need to become a draftsperson. You can do graphs by hand if you want, or on one of the many automated graphics programs such as the one included in many word processing and office suite packages. The intention of producing graphs is to provide yourself with a visual representation of the trend, not a work of art.

Computing an Average

In order to properly manage and track the trends you will identify, you will need to compute averages. The average helps to smooth out your graph so that the trend represents a general movement rather than an individual aberration. Without averages, trends often look like random and uncertain movements.

To demonstrate how averages help to clarify a trend graph, we will use the example of current ratio.

Example: You have tracked the current ratio over the past three years, with each quarter's ending current ratio listed as follows:

FIGURE 7.1 Scaling of Graphs

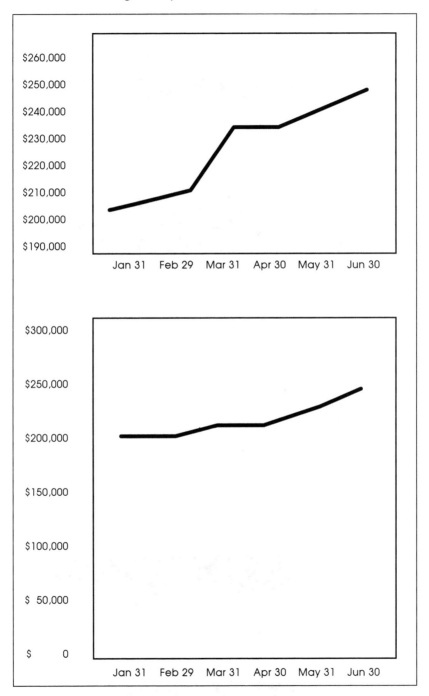

Period		Ratio
1:	year 1, first quarter	2.4-to-1
2:	year 1, second quarter	2.3-to-1
3:	year 1, third quarter	2.1-to-1
4:	year 1, fourth quarter	2.2-to-1
5:	year 2, first quarter	2.0-to-1
6:	year 2, second quarter	2.1-to-1
7:	year 2, third quarter	1.9-to-1
8:	year 2, fourth quarter	2.1-to-1
9:	year 3, first quarter	1.8-to-1
10:	year 3, second quarter	1.6-to-1
11:	year 3, third quarter	1.4-to-1
12:	year 3, fourth quarter	1.5-to-1

This listing of current ratios, by itself, would be difficult to interpret if that was as far as the trend analysis went. Figure 7.2 represents this history in scaled graphic form. Note that the ratio value of 2-to-1 is at the midpoint of the graph. This is the proper scaling for this ratio, because 2-to-1 is the standard. Any ratio at or above that level is considered positive; anything below that level is negative.

FIGURE 7.2 Current Ratio Trend

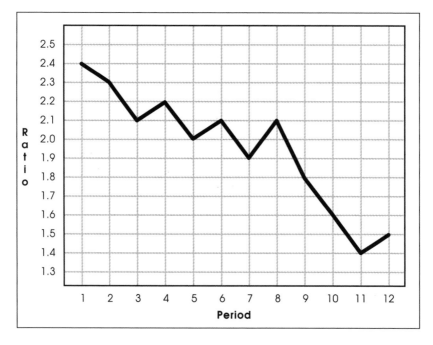

From this graph, you can see that the trend is negative. Clearly, the trend shows a deterioration in the current ratio over the past three years.

The trend would be clearer still if reduced to overall averages. The list of current ratios can be expanded to include the average current ratio for the entire period. The following is such a listing. The last column represents the average for the entire period being studied. Thus, the second period's average involves adding together the first two periods, and dividing by 2, while the twelfth period's average involves adding together all 12 periods, and dividing by 12.

Period		Ratio	Average
1:	year 1, first quarter	2.4-to-1	2.40-to-1
2:	year 1, second quarter	2.3-to-1	2.35-to-1
3:	year 1, third quarter	2.1-to-1	2.27-to-1
4:	year 1, fourth quarter	2.2-to-1	2.25-to-1
5:	year 2, first quarter	2.0-to-1	2.20-to-1
6:	year 2, second quarter	2.1-to-1	2.18-to-1
7:	year 2, third quarter	1.9-to-1	2.14-to-1
8:	year 2, fourth quarter	2.1-to-1	2.14-to-1
9:	year 3, first quarter	1.8-to-1	2.10-to-1
10:	year 3, second quarter	1.6-to-1	2.05-to-1
11:	year 3, third quarter	1.4-to-1	1.99-to-1
12:	year 3, fourth quarter	1.5-to-1	1.95-to-1

Note that as the averaged period increases, changes have less effect on the overall average. That is because with more periods being averaged, the latest entry's change has less overall influence on the total. It is safe to presume that, given a long enough field of values, the effect of a new entry would be minimal or nothing.

The effect of the overall average on the trend is shown in Figure 7.3.

The point about larger numbers of fields is shown here. Note that as the averaging period grows, the effect of a deteriorating trend is shown, but only minimally. Even so, the comparison between straight ratios and overall average makes our point dramatically.

⚷ KEY POINT

The larger the entries in a field to be averaged, the less effect each entry has on the overall average.

FIGURE 7.3 Current Ratio Trend with Average

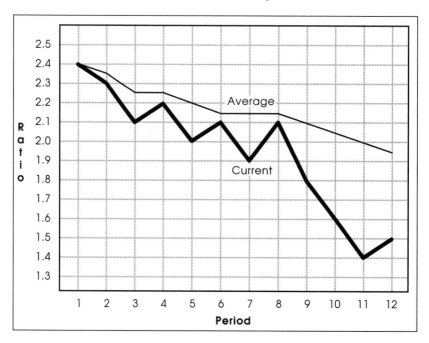

In this figure, we used a simple average. It involves adding together a field of values; there may be only two, or a dozen, or even hundreds. The total is then divided by the number of fields involved. As you saw in the previous example, the greater the number of entries in the field, the less impact the latest entry will have.

The formula for simple average is shown in Figure 7.4.

FIGURE 7.4 Simple Average

$$\frac{A + B + \ldots D}{N} = \text{Average}$$

$A \ldots D$ = Field of Values
N = Number of Values

FIGURE 7.5 Moving Average

1. $$\frac{A + \ldots D}{N}$$

2. $$\frac{(A + \ldots D) - A + E}{N}$$

Simple average is the kind of formula most people think about when they talk about an average. However, for the purpose of studying fundamental information over a period of time, simple average might not be the most efficient or reliable measure of outcomes. You do not desire the leveling out effect achieved with averaging when a large number of fields is involved. A volatile situation should appear volatile on your graph.

With this in mind, you will find it more convenient to employ a variation of averaging, called the moving average. This is a form of averaging in which the field size remains the same; and it is updated with each new value entry. As a new value becomes available, it is added into the field, and the oldest value is dropped off.

The formula for moving average is summarized in Figure 7.5.

The moving average involves two steps, as shown in the illustration. First, the initial average is computed by defining the field size; adding the values; and then dividing by the number of values in the field. Second, the oldest value is dropped off and the newest value is added on. In the formula, this is indicated by subtracting "A" and adding in "E."

Referring back to the list of current ratios, let's assume that you were to apply a moving average calculation using three periods. The calculation would be as follows:

Period	Ratio	Moving Average
year 1, first quarter	2.4-to-1	
year 1, second quarter	2.3-to-1	
year 1, third quarter	2.1-to-1	2.27-to-1
year 1, fourth quarter	2.2-to-1	2.20-to-1
year 2, first quarter	2.0-to-1	2.10-to-1

Period	Ratio	Moving Average
year 2, second quarter	2.1-to-1	2.10-to-1
year 2, third quarter	1.9-to-1	2.00-to-1
year 2, fourth quarter	2.1-to-1	2.03-to-1
year 3, first quarter	1.8-to-1	1.93-to-1
year 3, second quarter	1.6-to-1	1.83-to-1
year 3, third quarter	1.4-to-1	1.60-to-1
year 3, fourth quarter	1.5-to-1	1.50-to-1

In this example the average line would be dramatically different than that used for the simple average. You will recall that the simple average called for the use of divisors equal to the number of periods, so with a higher number of periods, there was a leveling out. Compare the average line in Figure 7.3 to that in the moving average, shown in Figure 7.6.

The average as represented in this latest version, using moving average, is more representative of what is occurring in the trend. For that reason, moving average is the more reliable method of the two.

FIGURE 7.6 Current Ratio Trend with Moving Average

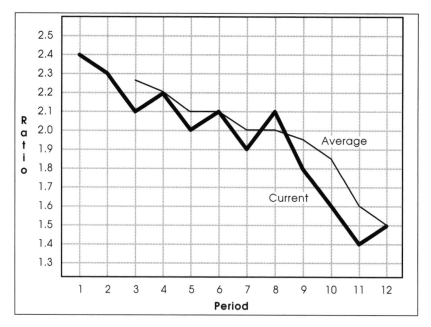

🔑 *KEY POINT*

The selection of a representative moving average is more useful than an overly large simple average.

Another consideration may be that, because the latest entry in the trend is more relevant, it should be given greater weight than older, outdated data. The justification for this belief is that with financial results, the latest information has greater relevance to the test of investment value. With this in mind, you can adjust the computation of average in many ways. The weighted moving average is a popular device in charting and in trend analysis.

One method involves first identifying the field to be tested in the moving average. For example, we showed what occurs with a moving average using a field of three values. Then weight the values according to your formula. You may give the latest entry a value of two, with older values each having a value of one. Then a field of three values would be divided by four. (The latest entry is included twice, so it adds another divisor.) Another method involves giving the current value a weight of 3; the second a weight of 2; and the oldest a weight of 1. Under this method, the total would be divided by six.

Referring back to the same example as before, the worksheet shown in Figure 7.7 can be used for calculating the weight, and then for doing the calculation.

The worksheet is set up for flexibility. Below are two renditions of weighted moving average, both using the previously introduced current ratio results. In the first example, weighting involves using only the latest three values. The most recent is given a weight of "2" while the others are given a weight of "1."

Period	Value	Weight	Weighted Value	Total
year 1, first quarter	2.4-to-1	2	4.8	
year 1, second quarter	2.3-to-1	1	2.3	
year 1, third quarter	2.1-to-1	1	2.1	9.2

The next step involves dividing the total by 4, which produces a weighted moving average as of the end of this period, of 2.3-to-1.

FIGURE 7.7   Weighted Average Worksheet

Period	Value	Weight	Weighted Value	Total

The second method calls for weighting the latest period with "3" and the second latest with "2," while the oldest is given a weight of "1."

Period	Value	Weight	Weighted Value	Total
year 1, first quarter	2.4-to-1	3	7.2	
year 1, second quarter	2.3-to-1	2	4.6	
year 1, third quarter	2.1-to-1	1	2.1	13.9

Next, the total is divided by six, for a weighted moving average of 2.3.

Monitoring Investment Return

Great emphasis is placed on getting the "inside track" and making a fast profit. In the stock market, the very idea of getting the jump on everyone else is, perhaps, the most alluring aspect of investing—for many, a primary motive for buying and selling stocks directly. In comparison, putting funds into a no-load mutual fund, reinvesting dividends, and forgetting about it, seems relatively uninteresting.

The real inside track—fundamental analysis—is not very exciting, at least in the short term. However, the rewards of gaining profits over time from the intelligent and informed selection of stocks, can be exciting as well as profitable. For this reason, it is important that you develop the means for measuring your market success. You cannot truly be aware of success unless you have a method for measuring it; and if you do not measure, then how else can you identify if or when you have succeeded?

In school, success is measured by grades. In the market, success is measured by profits. That means not only that you need to select companies that run their operations profitably, but also that are recognized and rewarded by the market. This is reflected in market price.

You cannot simply identify success as selling stock for more than its original purchase price. That is obviously better than selling at a loss,

➤ *KEY POINT*

Fundamental analysis is the ultimate "inside track" for the long-term investor.

but it does not establish any standard. You need to develop a method for measuring your own investment success. For this purpose, you may want to determine a method that defines success in your portfolio. The more this measurement is tied to market price, the more tendency you will have to be distracted by short-term price movement. The challenge is to identify a long-term measure of your success, without the recurring temptation to make investment decisions in response to short-term price movement.

One method worth considering is the annual yield approach. Set a goal for yourself concerning average annual yield you expect to earn from each investment. Remember, this is an average and might not be met each year. By setting the minimum standard, you will be able to better monitor your portfolio, and to determine if and when you will need to alter the direction you have chosen. This is the best method for even the long-term investor.

> **Example:** You have purchased shares of several companies, with the intention of building a retirement portfolio. The stocks were selected on the basis of several fundamental tests and you monitor results through ongoing trend analysis. One standard you set for yourself was a minimum annual average yield of 3 percent or more. This should be relatively easy to achieve, because the majority of your stocks cover about half that requirement through dividends. However, you have set a second part to this goal: If any stock fails to meet the average yield requirement after three years, you plan to sell and replace it with a different investment.

In this example, the goal is established and a means for monitoring and defining success is included in the mix. The three-year average yield requirement enables you to fine-tune the portfolio in the future, if and when a particular company's performance falls below minimum. In addition, your trend analysis should be designed to set minimum standards as well. For example, you might require certain performance-related outcomes tied to working capital, sales, debt/equity ratio, and any number of other tests—alone or in combination.

Can you equate investment success with corporate performance? You already know that the financial statement results do not necessarily mirror the market price of a company's stock, in fact, the perceptions of future value—a short-term market indicator—might frustrate the fundamental analyst in the illogic of the outcome. In the short term, there may be no relationship between corporate profits and perceptions of future value. In the long term, the two factors are tied together and cannot be separated. Of course the fundamentals ultimately affect stocks' market value. Perceptions are modified as future outcomes confirm or dispute forecasts.

There is a direct and inescapable relationship between a stock's market price and the fundamentals. However, that relationship is long-term. This is why the market price, as important as it is in the selection of a stock and in the decision to hold or to sell, does not mean as much today as most people think. If you plan to hold your investment for many years, then today's minor stock price movements should not concern you. As an investor, you will be interested in the performance of the stock, but market price alone is a tempting distraction that can easily cloud your judgment and make you forget about your long-term—and less exciting—investment goals. Don't overlook the importance of your trend analysis in determining whether or not your investments continue to meet a standard you have set. For long-term profits, that is more important than today's market price.

What to Look For in the Trends

The effective use of averaging makes trend analysis easier than it would be if the latest entry were merely placed on a graph. In the chaotic and random outcomes you will see in financial statements, it is difficult to predict what a single outcome means. You need the longer term—the *trend*—in order to fully understand what is happening.

Here are a few pointers in how to interpret trends.

* *Expect a leveling effect in growth trends.* Any measurement of growth will not continue to improve indefinitely. An improvement in sales volume or net margin (the two most common growth measurements) are limited in value except to the degree that they confirm rates of change; meet expectations; and satisfy anticipated outcomes within a range of results.

✦ *KEY POINT*

Make sure your expectations are realistic. Nothing improves at an ever-growing rate, forever.

- *Don't expect predictability.* Trends do not answer all of your questions, nor do they reveal a clear and unmistakable direction. The value of trends is that they reveal emerging tendencies; they do not provide you with a predictable means for knowing what will happen next.
- *Wait for confirmation.* Even when a trend appears to be changing in some manner, do not act on the information unless you have a second or third indicator from some other trend. No one trend should be enough to cause you to act.
- *Decide how you should react to a change in the trend; use performance standards.* Set goals for yourself that relate to your trend analysis. For example, you may set a minimum standard for a range of profitability; growth in sales volume; or maximum debt in total capitalization.
- *Constantly evaluate your base assumptions.* You select a base year on some premise, and that can change.

🏃 KEY POINT

Constantly question your own assumptions. Everything is likely to change in the future, even the best of your own assumptions.

- *Be willing to abandon a portion of your analysis.* Some trend studies end up being disappointing, or providing you with nothing of real value. Abandon analysis that is not providing you the insight you need.

🏃 KEY POINT

Flexibility is the most important attribute for long-term study of a stock. Just as companies change over time, so will the fundamentals that really show you what is going on.

Acting on the Information

The final step in this process is deciding what actions to take. The timing of decisions is critical, but that is more true for short-term thinking than for the more studied long-term approach fundamental analysts need to adopt. The game plan should approximate the following scenario:

- You invest in stocks after a detailed analysis of the fundamentals; a comparison among a field of likely candidates in specific industries; and a review of historical performance, financial strength, and return to shareholders.
- The purpose in buying stocks is long term in nature. You will not sell merely because you face an opportunity for an immediate profit, *or* because the stock's market price falls. All actions following the purchase of stock will be to maintain and monitor.
- The exception: when a trend changes. If a primary trend that led you to believe the stock was a worthwhile long-term hold were to change, you would consider selling. This will occur only when the trend is confirmed by other trends you watch.

This process is one that all investors may follow, assuming that the purpose in believing in fundamental analysis is because you already consider yourself a long-term investor. The market rewards shareholders. This is why the market is so popular, and why well managed portfolios are profitable over the long term.

In using graphs to map out trends based on ratio analysis, you have a three-part challenge. First, you need to ensure that you have selected the proper ratios for study. Watching the wrong fundamental indicators is of little value, so be prepared to switch from one form of analysis to another if your selected method does not work for you.

Second is the proper interpretation of results. As you begin to use moving averages and, perhaps, weighted averages when they add value to your study, you will become proficient at interpreting your trends, and you will be able to take action once information reveals itself.

Third, you do need to act on information—decisively and with confidence. Trust your decisions as long as they are based on the integrity of the underlying information, and you will not go wrong.

CHAPTER 8

Putting Market Services to Work

*I*f you read every financial newspaper and magazine, look for fundamental analysis on the Internet, use a brokerage company's research service, and subscribe to several investment newsletters, you will have a lot of information available, but you will spend all of your time reading. You must decide which information is valuable.

Because of the abundance of sources you want to be highly selective and develop your own conclusions from the study of a limited number of relevant ratios. However, you may also want to make use of a number of investment services, which provide a variety of information—everything from forecasts and opinions, through complete analysis of a company including in-depth fundamental analysis and trend reporting.

The Importance of Company Ratings

Many services rate company stocks in several ways. These are worth paying attention to because the ratings provide you with several important indicators of value, risk, timing, and performance. In future chapters, we will show you how to develop a rating system of your own, using a wide range of possible sources (including other rating services).

Below is a summary of two of the ratings you will find through subscription services, or that you will see referred to in analysts' reports. These are the most popular and useful services and both are affordable.

Value Line

This company has been in business since 1931, and is the best-known and most widely used investment service company. Several specialized services are offered by Value Line. One is the Value Line Investment Survey, a study of 1,700 publicly traded companies. Another is a condensed version of its survey, which analyzes 600 stocks.

The interesting feature of Value Line is its combined reporting of fundamental and technical indicators. The service is highly visual, including charts and tables for each of the stocks it studies. Value Line also rates each company for "timeliness," a ranking system it first introduced in 1965. The timeliness ranking is limited to short-term trading goals, and claims to indicate which of 1,700 stocks represent the best buys over the next 12 months, based on an evaluation of a broad range of indicators. For long-term investing, you still need to look to the fundamentals.

Value Line presents its subscribers with constantly updated information. In addition to the timeliness rating, it also provides a safety rating from 1 (highest) to 5 (lowest). Many other short-term and technical indicators are provided, including stock price movement charts, summary of price ranges, and projections for future growth.

In the area of fundamentals, Value Line gives subscribers updated breakdowns of a company's capital structure, working capital, growth rates, quarterly sales, earnings per share, dividends, price-earnings (PE) ratio, earnings predictability ratings, and financial strength. All of these are valuable as summaries of the fundamentals, and can be used alone to make decisions or incorporated into a program of your own design. Going beyond the numbers, these reports also describe the company's business as well as recent news, developments, and prospects.

At the very least, Value Line provides convenience. Information is updated regularly and each company is found on a single page. The survey is accompanied with statistical comparisons for all 1,700 companies studied plus industry analysis. This information is difficult to find elsewhere but extremely valuable when you are trying to determine whether to buy stocks in a particular industry or a particular stock in an industry.

To contact, write to Value Line, 220 East 42nd Street, New York, NY 10017; or call toll free, 800-833-0046. Web site: www.valueline.com.

Standard & Poor's

A competitor to Value Line, Standard & Poor's (S&P) produces research reports for more than 5,000 companies that are traded publicly. Each seven-page report is updated every day and subscribers can obtain them by fax or mail. Reports include recommendations, rankings, and an analysis of near-term profit potential, as well as numerous fundamental and technical indicators, including the same information provided by Value Line.

The stock reports and recommendations are based on S&P's stock appreciation ranking system, which calculates potential stock appreciation for the coming 6 to 12 months. As in the case of Value Line, short-term forecasts are not useful for long-term planning, but may add to your stock information sources. S&P ranks stocks and recommendations in five classifications: buy, accumulate, hold, avoid, and sell.

Another ranking of interest is the S&P quantitative model, which is a strength ranking based on both fundamental and technical indicators. Those stocks in the highest ranking, 5, are likely to perform better than the market average in the near-term; the lowest ranked, 1, are expected to do poorly.

S&P also provides subscribers with a fair value price, the price the stock should be selling for today. The company states that this ranking is based on earnings, growth potential, return on equity, price history, current yield, and other factors. In other words, this is a fundamental ranking, but estimates current stock price value.

A comparison between S&P and Value Line shows that both apply the same types of tests to arrive at rankings for safety and timeliness for each company—although they may use different names and descriptions. For example, S&P provides the same financial data as Value Line. Going beyond the numbers, S&P also provides a business profile, operational review, and a business summary—the same basic information as that provided by Value Line.

To contact, write to Standard & Poor's, 25 Broadway, New York, NY 10004; call toll-free, 800-221-5277; or visit the Web site: www.standardpoor.com.

The Financial Press

An ongoing source for market news—both fundamental and technical—is the financial press. This includes both newspapers and magazines, as well as dozens of useful newsletters. The major financial newspapers are described below.

The Wall Street Journal

This best-known and most widely circulated of the financial newspapers is published every business day. It includes complete listings for all public markets in the United States: stocks on the New York (NYSE), American (AMEX), and Nasdaq exchanges; options and futures listings; mutual funds; bonds; and market charts and indicators.

The *WSJ* also includes the most comprehensive financial news available, not only for United States–listed companies, but for economic and financial news worldwide. Some of the *WSJ*'s more interesting and valuable features include:

- *Earnings reports.* Summaries of latest-reported quarterly results for listed companies, including current and prior year results, showing sales, net income, number of shares outstanding, and net earnings per share.
- *Extensive news stories.* More than a financial paper, the *WSJ* also summarizes news affecting business and finance, including domestic and worldwide stories that investors need to know about individual companies, world trade and economics, political decisions, and industrial development.
- *Index to businesses.* This is a handy index of all listed companies, cross-referenced to stories in which those companies are named or quoted. This is a good way to keep abreast of news affecting companies in which you own stock.
- *Visual summaries of the market.* A chart showing activity in all three Dow Jones Averages includes index levels as well as volume for the past six months. Stories about specific companies often include sidebars showing price movement, sales history, or other indicators of interest.
- *Hourly breakdown of the averages.* The comprehensive stock listings are augmented by an hour-by-hour summary of the industrial, transportation, utility, and composite averages, for the past week.

- *Emphasis on key changes in listings.* The complete stock listings include visual highlights for specific items. Quotations in bold-face indicate a 5 percent or greater change from the previous closing price. Quotations underlined indicate significant changes in volume from past average volume.
- *New high or new low summary.* Each day's new high and new low levels for the past year are summarized in a sidebar.
- *Off-lot trading.* Summary of the activity of purchases and sales in lots other than 100 shares, believed by many to indicate significant changes in market trends.
- *Foreign market summaries.* Daily summaries of every major world stock market, including selected corporate names, closing price, and net change.

This paper is without any doubt the most comprehensive financial paper available. As a daily paper, it requires a considerable commitment to absorb all of its information on an ongoing basis, but few investors need to exercise that level of diligence. The paper is set up for ease of use, a format the Dow Jones Company has had more than 100 years to perfect.

To contact, write to *The Wall Street Journal*, 200 Liberty Street, New York, NY 10281; or call toll-free at 800-521-2170. Web site: www.dowjones.com.

Barron's

This is a weekly paper, also published by the Dow Jones Company. For those who do not want to pay for a daily paper, *Barron's* offers an acceptable and comprehensive weekly summary. It includes many of the valuable statistical summaries supplied by the *WSJ*, but with the perspective of a full week rather than day to day. For many, this is not only enough, but preferable.

Features include:

- *Editorials and opinion.* Many observations and opinion columns are included, such as "Up and Down Wall Street," "Review and Preview," "The Trader," "Trading Points," and "International Trader."
- *Index to companies.* Like the *WSJ, Barron's* includes a comprehensive cross-reference between companies named in stories and the page in each edition.

- *Feature stories.* Articles of interest to investors. Unlike the *WSJ*, which tends to emphasize news, *Barron's* includes stories of broader interest and with more information.
- *Summary, winners and losers.* This page includes interesting statistical summaries for the week, including biggest movers up and down, and most active in terms of percentage price change, share volume, and dollar volume. Statistics are provided for the NYSE, AMEX, and Nasdaq exchanges.
- *Instructions on reading stock tables.* Includes detailed explanations of stock ticker code symbols and market transaction symbols, enabling all readers—even novices—to grasp highly abbreviated listings conveniently and quickly.
- *Offer of free corporate reports. Barron's* offers free annual or quarterly information for companies, by displaying a three-leaf clover signal.*
- *Comprehensive stock listings.* The week's trading information is supplied for all exchanges, showing weekly activity rather than daily activity. This includes the NYSE, American, and Nasdaq exchanges, as well as foreign markets. Complete listings of bonds, futures, mutual funds, and other specialized markets are also provided every week, including valuable sidebars for major movers, volume in largest listings, and other information.
- *Market laboratory.* This section provides interesting statistical summaries and indicators, including half-hourly averages for the Dow Jones Industrial Average (DJIA) for the entire week; movement in all of the major indexes; advance and decline volume; block transaction summary; the PE and yield for indexes overall; new high and low price levels for the week; listings arranged by industry groups; a complete summary of economic indicators; dividend information, including payments, stock splits, and increases in dividend rates; trading suspensions and new applications to be listed; and name changes. In short, *Barron's* includes

---

* Free annual reports or quarterly reports can be ordered 24 hours per day by calling toll-free 800-965-2929, or by fax to toll-free 800-747-9384 (include ticker symbol and which report you are requesting). The same reports also can be ordered over the Internet at www.icbinc.com. *Barron's* also offers a free directory of reports currently available.

all of the useful fundamental, technical, and economic indicators for the week that you might want to accumulate and use in your own program.

The value of *Barron's* is in its comprehensive listings and the support it provides to investors in the form of statistical summaries, sidebars, highlighted and emphasized significant changes, and weekly overviews of market trends.

To contact, write to *Barron's* at 200 Liberty Street, New York, NY 10281; or call toll-free, 800-228-6600. Web site: www.barrons.com.

Investor's Business Daily

This west-coast competitor with Dow Jones publications stands up well in terms of financial news, statistical information, and market results. It is published every business day. Among its features are:

- *News summaries.* An easy-to-use, one-page section called "To make a long story short" provides readers with a glance at significant market news and trends.
- *Economic summary.* An in-depth summary of economic trends and news.
- *Industry-specific coverage.* Trends within industries, including visual summaries of industry revenues, leading companies, earnings, and special economic factors helping or hurting the industry.
- *Stock listings with extra indicators.* The paper includes a daily list, including highlighted NYSE 60 stocks showing the greatest increase in volume. Listings also provide information not given in other financial newspapers including: EPS rank, showing relative growth in earnings per share compared to other listed companies; relative price strength, ranking stock price stability compared to other listed stocks; changes in volume and price, ranked in comparative form; and a weekly industry group relative strength (Monday issues only). These indicators provide you with ranking mechanisms in addition to standard tests. They relate to price, volume, and stability for the most part, with some fundamental value as well.
- *Charts for stocks in the news.* A summary of the price, volume, and PE ratio shown in chart form for stocks hitting new high price levels. The visual aid helps you to see the relative indicators for these issues.

- *Coverage of other markets.* Like *The Wall Street Journal* and *Barron's*, this paper provides complete listings for all major exchanges and for mutual funds, bonds, and other listings.
- *Statistical summaries.* A daily summary of price and volume for all major indexes and markets; price levels on an industry-wide basis; 14 interesting psychological indicators; and comparative world stock market movements.
- *Company index.* A listing of companies mentioned in articles and cross-reference to the page.

Investor's Business Daily does not contain as much in-depth news as the Dow Jones papers. However, it is at least as visual if not more so, including numerous comparative charts for specialized markets and emphasizing price and volume trends.

To contact, write to *Investor's Business Daily*, 12655 Beatrice Street, Los Angeles, CA 90066; or call toll-free, 800-831-2525. Web site: www.investors.com.

Other Information Sources

One of the great benefits to participating in the American stock market is the abundance of high-quality information. You should never have reason to complain that it is difficult to find the information you need, that information is highly unreliable, or that a variety of opinions is not at your fingertips. The abundance also is a problem.

With such an abundance of information, your great challenge lies not in finding information, but in deciding which information to use, to rely on, and to incorporate into your program. In addition to the excellent financial newspapers available through subscription, in your local library, or on the Internet, you also can access numerous magazines and newsletters.

Magazines should be divided into several categories, because they do not all offer the same range of information. First are magazines published to emphasize corporate financial news. While discussion includes the fundamentals, the economy, and the stock market, the real emphasis is not on investing, but on how corporations are affected by changes in the economy, by politics, and by other domestic and international influences. These magazines are educational for broad overviews, but will not provide you with any specific information about fundamentals, investment skills and strategies, or insights into how the markets work—the kind of information most avid investors seek. These magazines may provide valuable background, but you should read them in your local library before deciding whether to subscribe. The most prominent among these are *Forbes* (800-888-9896 or Web site www.forbes.com) and *Fortune* (800-621-8000 or Web site: www.pathfinder.com/fortune).

A second category of magazines is the how-to classification. These magazines include those that offer investment advice and ideas from the highly technical to the trendier consumer-oriented publication. Typical features are profiles of average families and how they manage their monies, informative articles about specific investments, and basic consumer information for beginners. The list of magazines in this grouping is so long that none are listed specifically.

Yet another source worth considering is the newsletter field. Hundreds of investment newsletters are available and some services even offer trial subscriptions to dozens at a time, all for one fee. Generally, this method takes a lot of time and leads to little of real substance. Check the Internet, which itself might offer a more updated and informative source than any single subscription. However, some newsletters might provide you with valuable information, all depending on what you are seeking. Check with other investors, stockbrokers, financial planners, and other experts to determine which newsletters meet your exact needs. Find out about getting sample issues or a limited trial subscription, or find a copy at your library before subscribing.

Another potential source of fundamental information is the financial expert. This individual may be found using any of several names, such as financial planner, registered investment adviser, or stockbroker. Some financial experts might be able to supply you with the latest annual reports or financial statements for companies you are targeting; stockbrokers have access to the entire research department of their firm, which can be a valuable source for information.

A word of caution when using financial experts as sources: Remember that these individuals are paid for their services, either by a fee or, more often, on a commission basis. Thus, they make a living only if and when you execute a transaction. Even the best of commission-based salespeople cannot ignore this basic motive. You should never overlook this reality. Be especially wary if any adviser makes suggestions for how to invest without first knowing your personal financial situation, goals, and risk tolerance level. You should be in

✒ KEY POINT

Remember that most financial experts are paid only when you make a transaction. Be sure that you control the decision-making process, and that your ideas are more important than someone else's commissions.

charge of making your own decisions. People who try to pay someone else to make their investment decisions for them take the chance that they will not be well served.

The problems for many forms of research supplied through salespeople—even when it comes from a nationally known brokerage firm—is that the conclusions and advice often are geared toward short-term decision making. Emphasis is placed on forecasts of sales and profits levels, rather than insightful fundamental analysis. It comes down to the same problem every investor faces: needing the fundamentals but being distracted by technical analysis, guesswork, index watching, and the short-term prediction game.

Doing Your Own Research

Even if you use the various services and publications available, there is no magic wand that makes the task easier. Making money in the market is hard work. Persistence pays off over time, and so does patience. You will need to do your homework even with the best research available. It still requires reading. Some of the services, like Value Line and Standard & Poor's, make the job easier by supplying a vast amount of information in intelligently compiled formats. The daily and weekly newspapers are extremely well designed and provide every possible indicator you could ask for.

Check the following Web sites as potential sources for research or to link to even more extensive sources on the Web. Remember, though, that investing is one of the more extensive areas on the Internet. This list is by no means extensive, but is designed to lead you to further resources and links.

better-investing.org
busreslab.com

iw.zacks.com/library/lib.htm
pfinance.miningco.com
www.77investorlinks.com
www.aaii.org
www.cybertown.net
www.ey.com
www.finpipe.com
www.infoseek.com/Investing
www.investorguide.com
www.moneypages.com/syndicate/finance/general.html
www.moneymentor.com
www.moneytree.com
www.natcorp.com
www.scubed.com
www.seclaw.com/links/investorlinks.shtml
www.sites.com
www.thestreet.com
www.wsdinc.com

🏃 KEY POINT

Making money in the market is hard work. The real value of fundamental analysis is in providing a direction for the effort, not in showing you how to succeed without performing the work itself.

The real test of fundamental analysis—as you apply it in your own program—is not that it should be expected to provide you with information beyond what anyone else has, but rather to the degree that it helps you develop insight, confirm your beliefs, or discover information necessary to the decision-making process.

CHAPTER 9

How to *Really* Read the Stock Listings

With the emphasis on market price, investors—whether they believe in fundamental or technical indicators—are naturally drawn to the closing price and the degree of movement in the stock's market value. Because of that emphasis, it is easy to forget what is truly important in the stock market: the fundamentals and how each day's changes reflect what is happening with your investments.

The Basic Information

The typical stock listing varies with each financial publication. If you depend on your daily paper rather than one of the specialized investment-oriented papers, you probably get information about a limited selection of stocks—only stocks of regional interest or outdated information. If you subscribe to *The Wall Street Journal* or *Investor's Business Daily*, then you have complete listings available every day. If you subscribe to *Barron's*, you have a comprehensive weekly listing. And if you are on the Internet, you can get real-time quotes any time.

The advantage of using one of the specialized newspapers is that you get the complete listings for the New York Stock Exchange; American Exchange; Nasdaq; and nonstock listings such as mutual funds, bonds, options, futures, and foreign markets. For many investors whose portfolios are diverse, it is always desirable to be able to check everything

133

🐁 KEY POINT

Monitoring the entire market gives you greater insight than just watching the day-to-day changes in the stocks you own.

and not just the latest stock reports. The benefits of being able to monitor the entire market as well as your own portfolio cannot be emphasized too greatly.

Investors in the stock market have an added advantage if using the Internet. You may use this convenient communications medium not only to monitor stock prices, but to place orders, research companies, view current financial statements and news, and access economic and business news. The Internet is an important and powerful investor's tool and should be used for information gathering, at the very least.

To begin with stock listings: What do the daily summaries actually show? Each day's listings show a number of results for each listing company. Figure 9.1 shows a typical listing for Disney.

A good number of investors use a short-hand approach to reading stock tables. They find the company name and look at the far right column to answer the question: Did this stock go up or down today? This is an easy trap, because it is so visual and immediate. The day-to-day results, entirely technical, give you a quick method for scorekeeping that satisfies the urge to know—right away—whether this was a good day or a bad day on the market. The easiest way to judge this is to determine whether your investment capital is worth more or less than it was yesterday.

In the example provided, each share of Disney stock gained 43¾ cents. That is what a gain of seven-sixteenths means in terms of dollar value. So if you own 100 shares, you earned $43.75 on the day. What does this mean? If you are holding the stock for long-term appreciation, it means very little—not only because it is a momentary and rather

FIGURE 9.1   Stock Listing

52 weeks		Stock	Sym	Div	Yld %	PE	Vol 100s	Hi	Lo	Close	Net Chg
Hi	Lo										
100¾	68½	Disney	DIS	.53	.6	33	14756	96⅜₆	95¼	95⅛	+⅞₆

> ### ⚷ KEY POINT
>
> Don't make the mistake of using stock tables only to track daily price movements. There is much more in the stock listing than price change, and you need the range of information to properly monitor your investments.

minor change, but also because on a day-to-day basis, stocks go up and down in value. Information is relative, and value is relative as well. Of greater concern to the long-term investor is the determination of whether or not this particular company continues to represent an investment worth keeping. The daily stock listings provide some information, but not enough of the right information. This is yet another source of data that you can use as part of a larger program. As a stock market investor, you need to know how to read these listings, and not just the rise or fall on a daily basis.

Figure 9.2 expands the listing by explaining what each entry on the line shows. Each listing contains a lot of information that you can use for tracking and monitoring purposes. One of the pleasures of stock market investing is that you can watch your investment's value change from day to day. This is rewarding and exciting. In comparison, owning

FIGURE 9.2   Stock Listing with Explanations

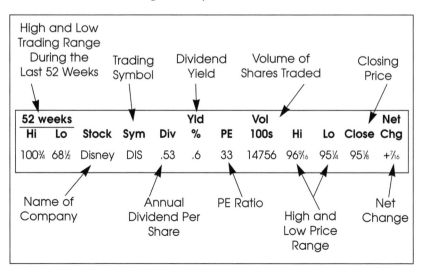

an investment like a piece of real estate is less satisfying because there are no daily listings telling you what your property is worth. It may well be that the broad-ranging popularity of the stock market is connected directly to this day-to-day reporting of higher or lower values.

What each segment shown in Figure 9.2 reveals about a stock is explained below:

- *High and low trading range during the last 52 weeks.* This is a summary of the price range over the past year. It lets you see, at a glance, the historical trading range of a stock. This shows not only the breadth of the trading range, but also that range in relationship to the stock's current price level.
- *Name of company.* The name or abbreviated name, the guideline being space. For example, the name Minnesota Mining and Manufacturing Company is too long to squeeze into the limited space; so in stock listings, this company is abbreviated as MinnMngMfg.
- *Trading symbol.* This is the symbol used in placing trades and reporting activity.
- *Annual dividend per share.* This is the dollar amount paid per share on an annual basis. If dividends are paid quarterly, the last four quarters are added together for this figure.
- *Dividend yield.* This is the portion of return on investment from payment of dividends. It varies every day as long as the market price changes, because it is calculated by dividing the latest reported annual dividend by the stock's closing price. The formula is shown in Figure 9.3. The result in the figure, .6, represents six-tenths of one percent.

FIGURE 9.3 Dividend Yield (rounded to one decimal)

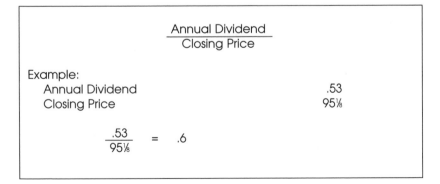

$$\frac{\text{Annual Dividend}}{\text{Closing Price}}$$

Example:
Annual Dividend   .53
Closing Price   95⅛

$$\frac{.53}{95\frac{1}{8}} = .6$$

- *PE ratio.* When you are reviewing and monitoring a stock, remember that everything is relative. This is true of the price-earnings (PE) ratio as with everything else. If you are monitoring a number of stocks, it is instructive to track the changes in PE ratio from day to day, and the differences in PE ratio from one stock to another.
- *Volume of shares traded.* This summarizes the day's trading volume in hundreds of shares. For example, the illustration shows volume of 14756. This means that 1,475,600 shares were traded that day. One indicator of market attitude toward a stock is to compare volume levels with trading range. As a general rule, you will notice that large price movements often are accompanied with exceptionally high volume; whereas little or no volume is reflected in slight movement in price. A company's stock shows great strength if its price trades in a relatively narrow range even with a heavy volume.
- *High and low price range.* This shows the day's trading range, which is useful because a comparison of breadth to closing price tells you whether the stock tended to rise or fall toward the end of the day. It further demonstrates market interest in the stock, especially when viewed in combination with volume levels. Also remember that each one stock has its own typical trading range and volume.
- *Closing price.* This is the most popular information for most investors, who want to know whether their stock went up or down today.
- *Net change.* This reports the change in stock price from the previous day's closing price to today's.

Putting the Information in Context

Each day's stock listing is the latest entry in a continuing trend. The listings should be viewed as such, and not as stand-alone results. For example, if a particular stock's market price rises two points today, it means that each share is worth two dollars more than the previous day. However, the price swings are not of as much significance as the longer term meaning of trends: if price sustains during downward turns in other stocks in the same industry; how the relationship changes between price and volume; how much breadth the price history shows; the dividend yield; and all of these things in combination, in comparison, and over time.

✦ KEY POINT

As with all indicators, information in the stock listings represents the latest entry in a trend. It should never be looked at without the perspective of what has happened in the past.

The very way that people tend to look at daily stock listings is flawed—mainly because they look only at the closing price and fail to study the overall information. If it helps, certain key trends should be tracked by placing information on a graph. A weekly or monthly summary will suffice, because entering a daily trend is tedious. Emphasis on the number of points in price movement also is inaccurate and does not provide any conclusive information.

Example: You are watching two stocks. Both rose three points yesterday. The first previously sold at $22 per share, and now is selling at $25 per share. The second previously sold at $51, and is now worth $54 per share.

At first glance, it would appear that both of these stocks performed equally well yesterday, because both rose three points. This is not an accurate conclusion. In fact, the lower-priced stock performed better than twice as well as the higher-priced stock, because the price movement represents a greater percentage increase. A three-point move from the base of $22 per share represents a rise of 13.6 percent. In comparison, the higher-priced stock, with a base of $51, grew only 5.8 percent.

Example: A comparison of last week's stock listings shows the results for two stocks you own. One previously sold at $48 and rose 4 points. Another previously sold at $19 and rose 3 points.

Most people would perceive a four-point rise as a more favorable result than a three-point rise. This is not entirely inaccurate, because each share of the higher-priced stock grew by four dollars per share. However, when making a percentage comparison, we see that the three-point rise represents a greater return from the previous week.

A four-point rise in the $48-per-share stock is an 8.3 percent return; and a three-point rise in the $19-per-share stock is a 15.8 percent return. The inaccuracy of point-watching is evident when you consider the amount of capital at risk.

Example: Two investors bought shares of stock. They each had $5,000. The first investor purchased 100 shares of a $50 stock, and the second bought 200 shares of a $25 stock. (These examples assume commissions are included.) They each held the stock for the same period of time, and sold on the same date. The first investor's stock rose seven points during the period it was owned. The second investor's stock rose four points.

Again, the popular method of evaluation is based on a point system, so the first investor's seven-point profit would be considered far better than the second investor's four points. But remember that they began with the same amount of money, and the second investor bought twice the number of shares. The real outcome of this example:

Investor	Initial Amount	Shares	Points Risen	Final Amount	Return
A	$5,000	100 at $50	7	$5,700	14%
B	$5,000	200 at $25	4	$5,800	16%

While the rates of return in this example are similar, the point remains the same: a smaller point rise is not necessarily a poorer outcome. If you evaluate the return on the basis of the amount invested, you discover that the yield is more significant than the point rise. Thus, a three-point rise on a $20 stock (15%) is far more significant than a 12-point rise on a $100 stock (12%)—especially if the identical amount of capital is invested.

✦ KEY POINT

Too much emphasis on point movement, to the exclusion of percentage change, distorts results and clouds what is really happening to a stock.

The day-to-day evaluation, while admittedly interesting, is also a distortion of reality. For example, an impressive-looking daily rise of nine points in a stock might be a recovery of the past week's 12-point drop. The matter of changing market values should not be reviewed in the short term, but as a part of the longer-term trend. Price ultimately matters because your profit will be determined by whether market price rises, but long-term fundamentals do not depend on daily price.

The way we view stock tables is flawed in yet another way. The comparison, with the great emphasis on the rise or fall from the previous day, is not centered on a logical base, but on the previous day—a relatively meaningless base. Of course, this is necessary because industry-wide reporting cannot have an identical base. You are interested in how your stock's price looks today, compared to the price you paid for it originally. In reviewing the daily or weekly stock reports, you do evaluate current price in comparison. However, in order to be completely accurate, you should also keep in mind the length of time you have owned the stock.

Example: You have two stocks in your portfolio. One stock was purchased only three months ago, and is currently about 3 percent higher than the price you paid originally. The second stock is 20 percent above purchase price, and has been in your portfolio for two years.

By annualizing the return, the comparison becomes a valid one. In the example above, it would appear that the second stock, which is 20 percent higher than purchase price, has performed far better than the first. However, in annualizing the return—expressing the return as though the stocks were both held for exactly one year—the outcome looks far different.

Stock	Period Held	Return	Annualization[*]	Annualized Return
A	3 months	3%	12 / 3 x 3%	12%
B	24 months	20%	12 / 24 x 20%	10%

The method of annualization shows that the second stock, with a 20 percent return, has not performed as well as the first stock—because of the time difference. Even this method of evaluation—comparisons between relatively short holding periods—does not provide you with the kind of yield information that is useful, especially if you intend to hold these investments over many years. Concern should be to ensure that the trend toward acceptable growth patterns is sustained, and not whether short-term yields outperform the market averages.

---

[*] To compute annualized return, divide 12 (12 months = one year) by the number of months in the period the investment was held, and multiply the result by the rate of return. In these examples, stocks were held 3 months and 24 months.

🗝 *KEY POINT*

The real performance of a stock has to be measured in the context of the length of time it has been owned. Otherwise, comparisons have no value.

Combining Volume and Price Information

Financial newspapers provide useful summaries of market activity in the form of a graph. One of the most valuable forms of graphs is one that shows information in comparative form, because in that way you are able to see how two related factors interact over time.

This is the case in overall comparisons between volume and price. For example, *The Wall Street Journal* reports a daily summary of the Dow Jones Industrial, Transportation, and Utility Averages, and the New York Stock Exchange volume—all for the prior six months. You can see at a glance the direct relationship between the levels of the averages and the volume of shares traded.

These are technical indicators, but they provide valuable information to all investors. As a believer in the fundamentals, you still need to keep in touch with the tone and mood of the market, and if nothing else, technical trends do reveal those features to you. Volume may do more. Besides showing how much immediate interest exists in the market, volume also shows the trading activity taking place. Keep in mind the fact that volume may be on the upside or on the downside. If a day's activity is driven by sellers, then downside volume prevails and prices will be driven downward. If activity is driven by buyers, then upside volume prevails and prices will be moved into higher territory.

Volume trends indicate the general direction of interest in the market. In periods when the market (as measured by the Dow Jones

🗝 *KEY POINT*

Volume is the thermometer of the market. It graphically demonstrates the excitement and enthusiasm—or fear and trepidation—ruling the market at any moment.

Industrial Average) is rising, volume may increase as well because more people are interested, and want to participate in the positive and, hopefully, profitable times. However, because the averages do not necessarily indicate real strength in the overall market, this is a dangerous tendency. Additionally, high volume might be caused not so much by individuals, but by higher interest among institutional investors. The largest volume of trading activity in the market takes place by institutions, and very little of the actual volume is represented by individuals, also called retail investors.

Although volume trends are instructive for the market as a whole, at least in gauging the current market mood, they should not be used as indicators for how you should act within your own portfolio. However, keeping an eye on the volume levels for a particular stock will be much more interesting, even when trends do not coincide with the market as a whole. Watching volume, you should concentrate on several tests, such as the following:

Volume changes over time.   As it is true with all trends, the test of changes over time is of the greatest significance. Changes in the volume of shares traded could indicate increasing or decreasing demand for the stock. Thus, watching volume trends can be useful for spotting an emerging change in a stock's popularity. A weighted moving average is recommended for following volume trends in individual stocks.

🔑 *KEY POINT*

Watching trends in volume may help you to spot changing perception of a stock, even before that change is reflected in the price.

Volume and price level comparisons.   Perhaps of even greater value than merely watching volume is comparing price and volume. This can be achieved by keeping a graph with two separate scales. It is helpful to be able to see changes of both price and volume together, because in some cases the technical trends are related to one another.

An example of a two-scaled graph for tracking price and volume is shown in Figure 9.4.

FIGURE 9.4 Two-Scaled Graph

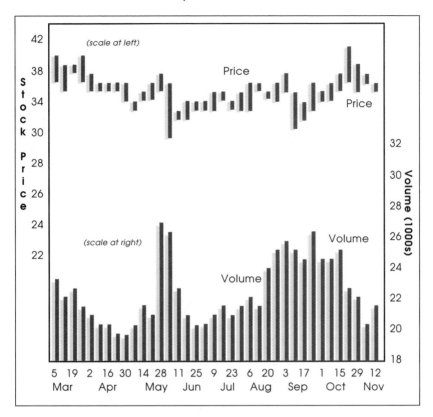

Volume and price breadth.   Another useful technical indicator to watch is the breadth of both volume and price—in other
words, the range. The more variation in these two factors, especially when viewed in combination, the less dependable the current
indicators. While you will be looking primarily at fundamentals, the
wider breadth of volume and price indicates greater than average
instability. If a relatively stable volume and price situation begins to
emerge, that may also be a sign of changing market perception
about the company. This could foreshadow a change in how the
stock will be viewed as a long-term growth candidate. For example,
if you purchased a stock when volume and price were stable and
since then the breadth is expanding, that could be a sign of long-
term price weakness.

🔑 KEY POINT

Stability in a stock's price can be measured by comparisons between volume levels and breadth of price.

A comparative study of volume and price can provide you with early warnings about potential problems with a stock. Even stocks held in high esteem today can fall out of favor tomorrow or in the next decade. If the fundamentals begin to change, thus confirming what market perceptions are already showing, then you might want to make a quick change in your long-term strategy. For example, your plans to hold stock could change suddenly to a sell decision—based on early signs in the technical trends showing up in volume and price, but confirmed by gradual and subtle changes in the fundamentals.

The Importance of Price Trends

The distinction between fundamental and technical indicators has to do with the source of information: financial results versus trading and price patterns. While fundamental analysis is scientific (in the sense that conclusions are based on fact), technical analysis is more intuitive (in that its premise is that market direction is predictable based on trends). To the believer in fundamentals, the technical approach lacks the logic and science that is so reassuring. However, some technical indicators—especially those used in combination with fundamentals, which we call technimental—can be very useful in portfolio evaluation and in market watching.

This is especially true when you are attempting to keep an eye on market risk—the best way to measure market risk is by testing the stock's tendency in relation to the market as a whole—in other words, its price movement history. Why is this valuable to those who follow the fundamentals? You should assume that price movement of a stock is a reflection of market perceptions, positive or negative, about the company. Those perceptions come from some form of information, which usually means information revealed in the fundamentals. So companies whose fundamentals tend to be less predictable also tend to have wider price swings. When analysts predict an outcome that is not confirmed by the fundamentals, the market price of the stock tends to react, often to overreact.

So price movement, while a reflection of immediate supply and demand, or of the market perception of value, is useful information. It is technical information that shows reaction to and perception of the company's fundamentals. Remember that price movement tends to be irrational in the immediate moment. Even so, it can be used as a means to measure market risk. This is important information about the fundamentals. Rock-solid companies whose profits and other fundamentals are predictable tend to have relatively stable market price. Companies whose fundamentals change drastically, whose fundamentals are difficult to predict accurately, and whose management is always in the news due to litigation, labor problems, product-related lawsuits, and competitive conflicts, are likely to have wider price swing histories.

The measurement of market risk is called volatility. This indicator involves subtracting the annual low price from the annual high price, and dividing the result by the annual low. The outcome is expressed as a percentage. The formula for volatility is summarized in Figure 9.5.

✒ KEY POINT

While market price is not a fundamental indicator, the tendency of a stock to trade in a broad or a narrow range is a good indication of market perceptions based on fundamentals.

FIGURE 9.5 Volatility (rounded to one decimal)

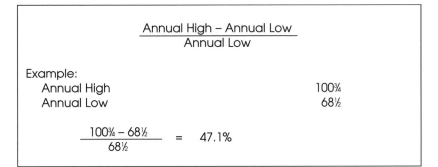

$$\frac{\text{Annual High} - \text{Annual Low}}{\text{Annual Low}}$$

Example:
Annual High   100¾
Annual Low   68½

$$\frac{100¾ - 68½}{68½} = 47.1\%$$

The greater the percentage, the higher the volatility of a stock. A relatively narrow trading range will produce a lower volatility percentage—thus less historical movement and less market risk—and a broader trading range will reflect higher volatility levels.

Volatility of the individual stock, as measured in its price range, is one way to define market risk. Another method is to compare an individual stock to the market as a whole. This measurement, called "beta," compares an individual stock price movement to the Standard & Poor's (S& P) 500 as a whole. The market beta is always 1.00, so that a stock's beta is compared to that index. If a stock tends to move more slowly than the S&P, then its beta will be lower than 1.00. For example, a stock with a beta factor of .75 tends to move below market tendencies. And the opposite is true as well; a stock with a beta of 1.25 tends to move more quickly than the S&P 500. Stock price movements, of course, may occur on the way up and on the way down. So beta measures movements, not necessarily profits.

Volatility measures market risk and opportunity, which are flip sides of the same test. The greater the market risk, the greater the opportunity. And the lower the market risk, the lower the tendency for rapid price appreciation.

🏹 KEY POINT

Risk and opportunity are flip sides of the same issue: a stock's tendencies to advance or decline in price.

Technicians consider volatility and the tracking of volatility trends to be extremely important, perhaps more important than actual price movement—because volatility defines the degree of market risk. Thus, it is also valuable to the fundamental analyst, because it defines market perception of a company as well as reaction to any news about that company. A variety on the measurement of volatility involves the market as a whole. By measuring and comparing advancing issues and declining issues, technicians can judge the price movement volatility of the market as a whole. Rather than being tied to price levels, this form of volatility tests the relative degree of price-advancing stocks to price-declining stocks. It is called the breadth index. It is computed by computing the difference between advancing and declining issues, and

FIGURE 9.6   Breadth Index (rounded to one decimal)

$$\frac{\text{Advancing Issues} - \text{Declining Issues}}{\text{Total Issues}}$$

Example:

Advancing Issues	1,106
Declining Issues	692
Unchanged	315
Total Issues	2,113

$$\frac{1,106 - 692}{2,113} = 19.6\%$$

dividing the result by total issues on the exchange. The result is expressed as a percentage. If advances outnumber declines, the result is positive; if declines outnumber advances, the result is negative. The formula for breadth index is shown in Figure 9.6.

The broader the gap between advancing and declining issues, the greater the breadth of the market. A higher percentage of breadth indicates an increasing tendency that day—tendency on the upside if advances outnumber declines, or tendency on the downside if the opposite is true.

These measurements tell you about the current condition of the market. With thousands of shares being traded each day, and with a mix of results, any one day's results rarely provide you the kind of insight you can get from trends in volatility and beta, or, for the market at large, in breadth of the market. As with all indicators, it is the general direction of the trend that counts, especially when a trend appears to be in reversal. Trend analysis is valuable only to the extent that it provides you with one of two forms of information: confirmation that nothing is changing, or a signal that everything is about to change—precisely the kind of information that every investor needs and wants.

Such insights cannot always be found in fundamental information alone. As a fundamental analyst, you cannot afford to ignore the technimental side of the market. It would be a mistake to discount entirely the value of some technical information. That would be investing in a vacuum. You will want to keep an eye not only on how a company's fundamentals change the investment value of the stock, but also on how market perception and mood affect all stocks in your portfolio.

> ### ✒ *KEY POINT*
>
> Ignoring technical indicators altogether limits your vision of the market. Some technical indicators give you insight into mood and, of utmost importance, might help you see an emerging trend before it becomes obvious to everyone else.

Volatility is a useful indicator to use in comparisons between several potential investment candidates. Volatility can further define whether a particular stock meets your risk profile. If you are seeking aggressive growth, higher volatility may be a requirement. If you are willing to accept steady but moderate growth over many years, then lower volatility may be more desirable. Comparisons of historical price appreciation and volatility reveal the connection.

Determining What You Really Earn

The test of profitability can be estimated from an accurate reading of the stock listings. The test of volatility provides a good indication of market risk, and the test of total return potential indicates the prospects for long-term yield.

Total return is the combination of dividend yield and change in price. Thus, you can evaluate stocks by comparing dividend yield alone—assuming that all have identical price appreciation potential. Because you cannot know the future of market price trends for a stock, this is a sensible way to eliminate investment candidates. The first step is to develop a list of stocks that have what you consider identical fundamental potential. The second step is to compare dividend yield to forecast future yield. Total return includes dividend yield, so a stock that pays little or no dividend may have a lower potential total return. However, a different argument may be made concerning dividends. Some companies argue that paying out dividends curtails the ability to reinvest profits to create future expansion, so nonpayment of dividends actually enhances future market price potential.

The decision to seek higher dividend income, or to ignore the value of dividend yield, has to be made individually. The debate over the real value of dividend payments cannot be settled conclusively. Some people invest primarily for dividend yield, with price appreciation a secondary consideration. Others put little value in dividends other than as indicators of continued management of profits. Some fundamentalists like to track dividend payments to ensure that a payment ratio is maintained over time. A reduced dividend or missed dividend would be a very negative sign. To some fundamental analysts, changes in dividend policies are far more valuable for fundamental signal value than the receipt of a dividend check.

CHAPTER 10

What Makes
Stock Prices Change

Supply and demand are at work in the stock market every minute it is open. Popular stocks will rise in value and unpopular stocks will fall. Popularity means that more people want to buy; their demand will drive up the price. You gain insights when you understand how and why a stock becomes popular.

Misconceptions about the Market

One attribute among stock market investors is a widespread belief that in some way, the market is predictable. More to the point, people want to believe that the future price of their stock choices can be predicted with enough reliability to ensure that they will undoubtedly make money. The desire to minimize the risk of loss—a legitimate concern—clouds judgment because, in fact, you cannot really predict with certainty which stocks will be profitable. So while a concern for risk is entirely appropriate, the methods for responding often are questionable.

If you apply a method of stock selection that is not logical or that is based on an interpretation of fact, then you have no right to expect consistent returns. Underneath all of the effort, you want to minimize the risk of loss. But if you don't believe in fundamentals, you need to use some other method. Technical indicators have such a large following because they are immediate, easy to understand, and reassuring. The belief that past trading patterns—whether viewed as statistical or visual—show the way to future price movement does not make sense to the fundamentalist. The accounting discipline tells us that economic forces determine the ultimate value of a company, that the value of a company creates the level of future earnings potential, and that future earnings potential determines whether a stock's value rises or falls.

✍ *KEY POINT*

Technical indicators are popular because they are immediate, they are easily understood, and they are reassuring. Even so, they do not provide you with the kinds of information you can only get from the fundamentals.

As logical as it is to follow the fundamentals, they do not spark the imagination of the average investor. Most people don't want to become analysts, and number crunching certainly is seen as a dry and uninteresting activity. The problem is figuring out how to use the valuable information that comes out of financial modeling and forecasting, without having to give up your excitement about the market. Unfortunately, widely held beliefs get in the way of sensible analysis. Be aware of the following popular myths among investors.

Market prices are predictable.   "Herd mentality" is frequently used to describe overall market thinking. The herd mentality is invariably wrong, as the belief goes. It is not always true, but there is a tendency toward widespread short-term beliefs to be wrong. Thus, highly popular stocks may be about to lose market value because—again,

✍ *KEY POINT*

Whether we like it or not, market price movements are not predictable.

according to this theory—by the time the "average" person believes, along with the majority, that a particular stock should be bought, it is already too late. In fact, you should do exactly the opposite of what the majority believes. If you subscribe to this theory, you are a contrarian.

Stock prices will continue going up indefinitely.   Stock market investors are most often optimistic. This is reflected in the way financial news is reported. Listen carefully. When the market rises, it is a rally. The news is expressed in the most positive terms. But when the market falls, it is rarely reported in pessimistic tones, unless the fall is dramatic. Moderate falls are characterized as consolidations, reactions, or other cautiously phrased occurrences.

⚡ KEY POINT

Nothing continues to rise forever. Even the most optimistic point of view has to allow room for the inevitable downward turn at some point.

Today's price represents a low price.   When investors first consider the market, they make the mistake of assuming that the current price of a stock represents the starting point, the low, the line against which future profits will be measured. Starting out on the premise that the current price is a low price is a way of assuming that once you buy the stock, it has to go up—because you are investing to make a profit.

⚡ KEY POINT

Stock prices might move in either direction, often for reasons that cannot be predicted—or for no apparent reason at all.

The worst risk is missing the immediate opportunity.   Many people fall into the trap of buying impulsively, out of a fear that they will miss an opportunity. This leads to poor decisions because real opportunities are found in long-term trends (fundamentals), and short-term price movements are just that—short term.

Prediction-making has intrinsic strategic value. Because so much effort is put into making predictions about overall averages and market trends, it is easy to fall into the mistaken belief that future prices and tendencies are predictable.

> ### ⚒ *KEY POINT*
>
> Forecasting future price movements is a form of psychic activity. Many claim to have been right in the past, but the past, we must remember, is much easier to predict.

There is only so much capital, so winners and losers off-set each other. One of the most baffling beliefs in the market is that for every winner, there is also a loser. This belief comes from the assumption that the free economy operates on a finite amount of capital.

> ### ⚒ *KEY POINT*
>
> It is the nature of the capital market that profitable business activity actually creates more capital. This is where the real potential of the stock market exists for the average investor—buying into the stock of a strong growth candidate.

The Random Walk Theory Applied

The random walk theory states that price changes are not related to market forces but are based on the random application of new information. History disputes the random walk theory. Well-managed companies with track records for controlling markets, producing profits, and rewarding shareholders contradicts the theory entirely.

The random walk theory is not really entirely random, however. The extreme application of the theory is fatalistic and cynical, assuming that price movement is arbitrary. But a more moderate point of view makes a clear distinction between "random" and "arbitrary." If market forces did not work in the market at all, then the extreme version of the random walk theory would apply. However, the random walk theory is somewhat more scientific than that.

🔑 KEY POINT

In terms of the random walk, *random* is not the same thing as *arbitrary*.

Order and sense do exist in the market, although short-term actions, reactions, and price movements themselves might not indicate that this is so. The real order and sense of the market exists in a long-term sense. The forces that affect stock price movement and that create varying levels of change in supply and demand, are in fact fundamentally based. You can believe in the random walk theory insofar as it applies to charting price movement, and still have great faith in fundamental analysis.

🔑 KEY POINT

You will not find order, sense, or logic in the market if you only watch the day-to-day responses and price movements. Those attributes are buried deep in the fundamentals, which is where you will profit in the long run.

Even if you have utmost faith in the fundamentals, some information developed by chartists can be useful to you. Specifically, the concept of support and resistance can be used as a form of technimental analysis. The chartist contends that support and resistance are absolute trading ranges, at least until a breakout occurs.

For you as a fundamental analyst, support and resistance levels may be thought of as the equivalent of real estate prices in a residential housing market. In your town, a typical three-bedroom house has certain predictable features and sells within a well-known range of price.

If you study that market, you can get to the point that you can estimate housing prices with a fairly high degree of accuracy. However, even given that current condition, at some point in the future prices will begin to change. In a good economy, people will want to move to your community, and the new demand will drive prices up—a breakout on the upside. But if more people are leaving town, demand falls and an oversupply may lead to a downside breakout.

This basic supply and demand scenario can be applied in the stock market as well, although the changes tend to occur with greater rapidity than in the housing market. For now, a trading range can be established for a specific stock. It is defined by support and resistance levels. The price is unlikely to fall below the support level, or to rise above the resistance level—for the moment. This defines the current conditions for that stock.

With this information in hand, you can make informed decisions in the short term. The stock's chart might indicate not only the support and resistance levels, but the historical length of time that those levels hold before a breakout occurs. Remember, these historical indicators cannot be used to predict the future reliably—they show only past patterns. While a chart might serve as one source for information, you should also remember the basic theme of the random walk theory: Stock prices have no memory.

The Auction Marketplace

The stock market operates on risk. Some people are rewarded by taking the right risks at the right time, while others make the wrong move and lose. However, while risk is the real determining factor, the public image of the market is that forecasting makes the real difference.

An investment strategy based on the fundamentals can be more profitable than average if you understand that for whatever reasons, the market has undervalued a company or its industry. The selection of decision-making strategies based on fundamentals and careful observation of the market may involve the combined strategy of looking for undervalued securities, with a thorough and logical program of fundamental analysis. Are the two compatible? They may be at times, but not always. For example, there may be fundamental reasons that some companies are undervalued by the market. Remember that in the auction marketplace, it is not today's value that counts for much; rather, it is the perception of potential future value that determines the popularity of one stock over another. Because perceptions drive the market, it is necessary to look for the source of perceptions. Invariably, long-term perceptions grow from the fundamentals.

🔑 KEY POINT

The important perceptions—those that operate over the long term—are outgrowths of underlying faith in the fundamentals.

It is not inaccurate to define market perception as a form of broad wisdom. You might not be able to find a particular analyst who can pronounce what the market believes about a stock. Perception is an unspoken judgment, passed on a stock by the market as a whole. It is wisdom without consciousness. Thus, a comparison between the workings of the auction market—driven by perception and short-term forecasting—and the traditional beliefs about fundamentals and future value, will not always yield complete consistency. However, you will probably come to the conclusion that perceptions accurately represent the broad wisdom that comes from a study of fundamental indicators.

You may equate perceptions with fundamentals or accept perceptions as a form of general fundamental understanding about a company's financial strength. But that is only part of the equation. A perception may be held by a person who knows nothing about fundamentals, does not review financial statements, and does not trust historical information. Such a person does not have an instinctive grasp of the fundamentals. However, he does have an instinctive awareness of the perceptions around him, and he has been able to pick up that sense and apply it to the stock in question. That is how herd mentality is born.

🔑 KEY POINT

Perceptions might come from analysis or from duplicating the attitudes and beliefs of others. It is difficult to tell just by observing, because perceptions look alike regardless of their source.

When investors form opinions based on their reading of perceptions around them, those opinions may be correct, but they are based on what others think. In the long run, successful investors usually end up either thinking for themselves or changing their source of information or opinion.

Supply and Demand in Action

With the emphasis on charting and other technical indicators having nothing to do with economic factors, it is easy to ignore the hard realities. The Dow Jones Averages do not measure any economic influences, nor are they based on anything except unweighted prices in a few stocks. We have previously detailed the problems of the Dow Jones Averages. However, the averages are so widely depended on and reported, and they are recognized as "the market." Therefore, the very important influences of supply and demand may be overlooked.

Most people understand the basic theory of supply and demand. However, a brief and simplified review is in order. As demand grows for a particular stock, its price is forced upward and, as demand is lowered, prices will fall. This generalized observation of the economics of the market applies in virtually all free markets, from grocery stores to auto lots to appliance outlets. But what is less understood is the reason for changing levels of demand. Why do people suddenly want to buy a particular stock, and of equal interest, why do people want to sell?

⫣ KEY POINT

You might understand the theory of supply and demand, but knowing about the nature of these changes is rather mundane. We know the answer to the question: What is demand? A more interesting question is: Where does it come from?

Following are a variety of apparent reasons, and a few not so apparent ones, why demand for a stock fluctuates.

Institutional investors have a lot of influence.   Remember that the majority of trade volume on the public exchanges is the result of institutional trading (mutual funds, etc.) and only a small portion consists of individual traders.

Forecast results do not always come to be. Great reliance is placed on professional analysts' forecasts. The entire theme of the market is speculation about what the future will hold. If a forecast is not met, even though returns may be acceptable. some investors decide to sell.

Rumor and speculation are taken seriously in the market. You may understand the theory of supply and demand quite well. But after observing the market for a while, you will come to see that rumor and speculation count for much more than fact.

The herd mentality makes the market irrational at times. When a mass of people come to believe something, even if it is not true, they all act as though it is true. So they may buy or sell based on that belief.

🏃 KEY POINT

You may be frustrated by the illogic of the herd mentality. However, it should be enough to observe it and to learn from it without giving in to its influence. This is a valuable form of market intelligence.

Fundamentals, while respected, are pushed aside when more appealing arguments are available. A certain financial position and financial results are factual data, especially when confirmed by independent audit. If you ask fellow investors or read what professionals say, virtually everyone has great respect for the fundamentals. But the actions of the market are based on less rational information, and on factors having no economic base.

Some historical changes in supply and demand have been entirely irrational, even hysterical. You can learn a lot about the modern stock market by looking at historical examples of market irrationality. The most extreme has to be the seventeenth century events in Holland concerning the market for tulip bulbs. A market appeared suddenly for rare tulips and many people were able get rich in the short term by speculating in those bulbs, not only in Holland but in other European countries as well. As activity increased, more and more people came into the market, driving prices up. Greed took over. Historian Charles Mackay in 1841 noted that in *Extraordinary Popular Delusions and the Madness of Crowds:*

> ... it was deemed a proof of bad taste in any man of fortune to be without a collection of [tulip bulbs] ... The rage for possessing them soon caught in the middle classes of society, and merchants and shopkeepers, even of moderate means, began to vie with each other in the rarity of these flowers and the preposterous prices they paid for them.

As it always happens in such situations, the bottom fell out of the market without warning. Bulbs worth four thousand florins fell quickly to three hundred, and even at that price, no buyers could be found. Fortunes were ruined.

✦ KEY POINT

To become truly wise in the market, learn the basic lesson of history, especially as it applies to markets, to the nature of greed, and to how to avoid making basic errors.

Is the Market Efficient?

Like all theories, the efficient market theory deals in absolutes. Logical minds know that absolutes rarely exist, and that the value of a theory is to represent one point of view. The troubling thing about the efficient market theory is that, if it is true, then all selections of stock are 50–50 propositions. Because it says that all known information is reflected in the price, we cannot know whether immediate changes in that price level will be positive or negative.

Resistance to the idea of depending on fundamentals for long-term successful investing comes from the desire to make a profit as quickly as possible, and with the least amount of work possible. This is human nature. Given two courses, people tend to take the easier as long as the end result is the same. However, in the market the end result of taking what appears to be an easier course might not be the same. The truth is, many investors choose to ignore risk. They tend to see potential for profit, while ignoring the equal and offsetting risk of loss.

This problem becomes evident when markets go through long periods of rising levels in the Dow Jones Industrial Average (DJIA). Remember, the point value of the DJIA has no real meaning, other than as a measurement of what is perceived to be the market now, versus where it was yesterday. The DJIA is a means of measurement that has no basis in supply and demand; in economic reality; or in the fundamentals of companies listed on the New York Stock Exchange. However, a run-up in the Dow like the one seen during the 1990s, leads many people into the market for the first time. As long as the DJIA continues upward and as long as investments made by these first-time players continue to climb, there appears to be no risk of loss. Everything moves upward without fail. Invariably, when a correction occurs or when the mood swings to the opposite direction, these first-time investors are caught off guard.

🏃 KEY POINT

The only value in the Dow Jones Industrial Average point level is that it offers a means to determine when the perception of the market is off.

This occurred when the big correction of October, 1987 took place. It will happen again in the future. If it were possible to warn people in advance about the risks associated with investing—notably the short-term risk, where most of the action takes place—people might take a more cautious view or, in the alternative, they might end up adopting the long-term position based on fundamentals, which is the more mature approach to the market. However, one of the problems in the market is that professionals are geared to the short term just like most people. Professionals want to be believed, and they want their customers—investors, subscribers, clients—to believe in their advice and expertise. Thus, professionals have little incentive to try and damper the enthusiasm of investors. To the contrary, the greater the enthusiasm, the greater the professional's perceived indispensability in the scheme of things.

You cannot expect to make a profit in the market by knowing what is going to happen short term, because you cannot know. You are rewarded for taking the right kinds of risks and for being patient. If you select stocks based on the fundamentals and combine the fundamental information with certain technimental indicators, you will be in a much better situation than most individual investors. You cannot depend on forecasts to ensure profits, because forecasting is extremely imprecise. Even a generally correct forecast can deceive you short term.

Regardless of what theories you follow or what observations you make about the herd mentality of the market, you invariably return to dependence on the fundamentals. Your investing approach requires three steps in order to succeed, none of which have anything to do with current price levels. The three steps are:

1. *Get the information you need.* The successful investor does not act on market price alone, because price is only today's perceived value of a stock.

2. *Decide on the most appropriate strategy.* The approach you take with your portfolio depends on your own goals. Investors are different, and no advice given to you by someone who does not know you can be trusted.

3. *Identify the associated risks.* The risks of investing are as important as the potential, because the two cannot be separated. Higher potential means higher risk, and lower risk is accompanied by lower potential. This is the nature of investing, whether in the stock market, in real estate, or in tulip bulbs.

Beating the Averages

Performance is measured against the market as a whole, which is appropriate because we need to have some method for judging success. In school, the criterion is well understood. A passing grade is easily quantified by meeting the goals of the course, by attendance, and by test performance. In the market, the criterion is not always as clear.

What is the market? Obvious choices include measurement of indexes and averages, but perhaps a more valid approach for you would be to compare your portfolio's average annual yield to that of other investment choices, such as your local real estate market, savings accounts, or mutual fund investing. The most popular way of getting into the stock market is through buying shares of mutual funds, so if

🔑 *KEY POINT*

Be sure that you measure your success against a valid standard, even if you have to come up with one of your own. Don't overlook comparisons of risk in the equation.

your fund outperforms the market (in whatever way that is measured), then you have achieved a degree of success.

The problem with any form of comparison is that risks are not always comparable. A comparison between the stock market and real estate involves many different risks: market forces move at different rates, real estate lacks the liquidity of the stock market, and you have more direct control in managing property. In other words, these are not comparable markets because the risk factors are vastly different.

In view of the fact that market prices change for a wide variety of reasons—none of which have much to do with long-term strategic planning—the questions you should be asking are not tied to price. Developing a good understanding of what causes price changes is inherent in becoming aware of your market.

CHAPTER 11

Economic Indicators *or* Gauging the Economy

Some forms of financial information are more public than others. Everyone has heard about economic indicators—changes in national trends relating to growth, the value of money, investments, employment, and inflation.

What affect do these various indicators have on your investment portfolio? With great emphasis on market prices of stocks and related technical trends, it is easy to overlook the fact that stocks represent equity in corporations. Those corporations and their future profits and losses depend largely on how they ride out the business cycles that all business enterprises face. So you cannot consider the market value of stock without also considering how that company will be affected by economic indicators. Some industries, for example, tend to be sensitive to interest rates. So, if interest rates rise, the public utilities industry is likely to experience lower profits, because they tend to use long-term debt capitalization to fund many capital projects. Other industries tend to have volatile cycles tied to inflation, money supply, and employment statistics. If you invest in a particular industry, you should want to become familiar with that industry's particular sensitivity. For example, consider the relationship between money supply and the financial services or real estate industries, between inflation and technology, and between employment trends and manufacturing.

The Business Cycle

The study of business activity in a free enterprise system invariably includes discussions of cycles. At some points in a cycle, business is robust and demand is high; at others, business is very slow and demand is low. Cycles are of great interest to forecasters because they are highly predictable. And because forecasting requires some idea of what is to come in the future, the ability to anticipate cyclical change is extremely important.

A business cycle is not a simple thing. It consists of many component parts and many variables. Just as you may use fundamental analysis to spot gradually changing trends in key company-specific financial data, so a study of national economic indicators is also a study of trends. Overall trends in the economy will have an effect on specific industries, and thus on the companies in those industries.

The challenge for the economic indicator forecaster is predicting not whether a cycle will occur, because it will, but identifying the point at which specific changes will occur. In other words, it is all a matter of timing. Analogies to the management of an investment portfolio continue to apply. If you know that a particular stock is likely to increase in value, it matters if you buy that stock at the beginning of its growth potential, or at a momentary price peak. Like individual companies, the economy is also cyclical.

✎ KEY POINT

Business cycles are predictable in their patterns, but not in the timing of events. No one can say how long a cycle will last.

In simplistic terms, the stock market reflects a sort of economy. For those familiar with the definitions of markets, the following review is unnecessary; for others, the purpose is to demonstrate the importance of economic indicators to the stock market and to individual stock investments. A bull market describes a positive, upward-trending market, in which investors can expect higher profits from buying and holding stocks; and in which the Dow Jones Industrial Average (DJIA), Standard & Poor's (S&P) 500, and other popular indexes are going up. In a bull market, companies are turning in earnings reports that meet and surpass forecast levels, usually because the overall economy is strong; inflation is low; unemployment is low; and the demand for the goods and services being produced is at a healthy level. Increasingly, bull markets also indicate healthy international trade levels and monetary exchange rates. When a pessimistic mood prevails over a period of time, that is called a bear market, characterized by falling stock prices and short-term losses.

✦ KEY POINT

The stock market reflects the economy of the business community. The attitude among investors reflects the market as a whole's opinion of the economic health of the business community.

One of the never-ending questions among investors, market-watchers, and analysts is: What causes economic changes, bull or bear markets, and other cyclical changes? In the free enterprise system, one of the interesting aspects of investing is the uncertainty of business cycles. The truth is, no one really understands the reasons that cycles occur, their timing, or why capital markets react as they do. Many theories abound, but no one really knows. The problem is perhaps best summed up by George Bernard Shaw's observation: "If all economists were laid end to end, they would not reach a conclusion."

Looking Beyond the Company's Numbers

It is appropriate to consider national economic indicators as a form of broad fundamentals. In studying the fundamentals of a particular company, you are probably aware of numerous causes for the current condition of a company. These include: quality of management, level and quality of service, diversification, industry position, reputation (of the company and the investment quality of its stock), dividend and earnings record, and other related factors. However, the financial strength and results also are affected by outside influences, including interest rates, unemployment, money supply, inflation, and other economic indicators. These cannot be ignored.

Just as investors should remember that the market price of a company's stock is not the same as that company's financial performance, it also is important to recognize that the influences on such matters as corporate profits are rarely internal only. Outside forces play a role as well. And corporate management decisions cannot influence the overall economy, whereas the overall economy clearly will affect the future profits of that corporation.

🗝 KEY POINT

The influences on corporate profits are rarely internal only. Many outside factors also determine a company's profitability and financial strength.

The financial press provides good summaries of key economic indicators, and a review of these is worthwhile for long-term monitoring as well as short-term forecasting of a corporation's profits. Because economic indicators are broad and apply nationally, it is difficult to equate changes in the indicators to a particular stock investment. However, a larger investment view—a world view, perhaps—is essential to successful investing.

Because the value of your portfolio will be affected by changes in economic health of the nation, you need to know how such matters are changing. It is the nature of economic cycles to take us by surprise. It is rare that an analyst accurately forecasts and pinpoints significant changes in economic indicators. While such changes will occur, no one really knows when. Every cycle has its own timing and rhythm and no two cycles can be depended on to duplicate the same pattern. What might look like a changing trend right now could be nothing more than a brief deviation in the trend, a blip contrary to the real direction that an indicator is moving. This is why hindsight is much clearer than foresight.

🗝 KEY POINT

It is not easy to pinpoint changes in cyclical trends. The trend lines rarely provide clear signals except when reviewed much later. Explaining the past is always far easier than predicting the future.

Valuable Indicators and Where to Find Them

One of the best places to find all of the important economics indicators is in the "Market Laboratory" section of the weekly paper *Barron's*. Here, the important indicators are summarized together in a two-page summary. The advantage of a weekly review of this type is that it enables you to scan the entire range of important indicators. It is rare that a single indicator will provide you with a snapshot of national economic health with more clarity than reviewing all of the indicators at the same time.

✒ KEY POINT

A review of a range of economic indicators provides insight into the economy in general, whereas a single indicator, reviewed in isolation, is not as valuable.

You may be interested in only two or three indicators, and it is a certainty that some have gained more attention than others in the minds of investors. Among many investors whose interest is more toward technical analysis than the fundamentals, economic indicators seem remote, indeed. This has given rise to many generalizations about the meaning or importance of economic indicators. In practice, though, they are just that: indicators. Like the fundamentals of a company, economic indicators provide general ideas about the state of things, and not absolutes.

Stock market participants usually are particularly concerned about changes in interest rate levels, anticipating the inflow or outflow of investment dollars between stocks and bonds, or between the stock market and other markets. There is more, and some indicators influence some industries more than others.

Below we will discuss key indicator ranges of inflation, employment levels, money supply, interest rates, national debt, business and economic measurements, and stock market and investor sentiment.

Inflation

The significance of inflation in the stock market should not be overlooked. For investors, the idea of rising prices has two separate meanings.

First, it means that goods cost more; second, it means that the value of investments potentially changes. Inflation is normally reported in percentage terms, meaning increases or decreases (deflation) from one period to another. This change is reported nationally as the Consumer Price Index (CPI), which is computed and published by the Bureau of Labor Statistics. The CPI is a combined index made up of major groups, which include consumer expenditures for food and beverages, housing, apparel and upkeep, transportation, medical care, entertainment, and other goods and services. The most commonly cited index is properly called the CPI-U, or the Consumer Price Index for All Urban Consumers. This encompasses the spending of approximately 80 percent of the U.S. population. The second of the two indexes is the CPI-W, or Consumer Price Index for Urban Wage Earners and Clerical Earners, which reports on spending for approximately 32 percent of the U.S. population. The CPI is an important economic indicator because it tracks and reports the changes in prices of goods and services purchased in urban households. (For more information about inflation, the CPI, and the Bureau of Labor Statistics, connect to Web site: stats.bls.gov.)

🔑 KEY POINT

To investors, inflation means not only that prices rise, but also that the profitability of their investments might change as well.

Inflation often is misunderstood as causing prices to rise when, in truth, it is the outcome of rising prices. The economy is a complex interchange between goods and services and consumer demand. Corporate price increases reflect higher prices of raw materials, labor, and other costs and expenses for the corporation; it is not the act of raising prices that causes inflation. In the August 1, 1967, issue of *Forbes*, Roger Blough stated: "Steel prices cause inflation like wet sidewalks cause rain."

The relationship between inflation and the stock market is direct, because as the rate of inflation grows, it is seen as a negative factor for corporations. Inflation affects business in general and usually indicates higher interest rates as well as prices, meaning ultimately less consumer spending. The consequence is lower sales and profits for the corporation. So watching the rate of inflation is relevant to investment climate as well as to the standard of living in all American households. Investors observing the long-term effects of inflation also realize that the real test of investment success is its ability to outpace inflation over time. You really stay ahead of inflation if you can beat its rate on an after-tax basis.

Inflation is reported in the form of a changing index, based on a starting point of 100. Each period's reported change has a value related to this starting point. A typical report shows the latest data is compared to the level the year before, and a rate of inflation is computed. A typical report shows two lines: Consumer Price Index and rate of inflation.

Inflation	**Latest Date**	**Latest Data**	**Preceding Period**	**Year Ago**
Consumer Price Index	Dec.	161.3	161.5	158.6
Rate of inflation (%)	Dec.	1.7	1.8	3.3

The rate of inflation is computed by first figuring out the change between the current CPI and last year's CPI; and then dividing the change by last year's CPI. If the rate is lower, the change is reported as a negative. The formula for reporting the rate of inflation is shown in Figure 11.1.

FIGURE 11.1 Rate of Inflation (rounded to one decimal)

$$\frac{\text{Current Inflation Index} - \text{Prior Year's Inflation Index}}{\text{Prior Year's Inflation Index}}$$

Example:
Current Inflation Index   161.3
Prior Year's Inflation Index   158.6

$$\frac{161.3 - 158.6}{158.6} = 1.7\%$$

Employment

A second indicator of great importance in the stock market is the employment rate. Many corporations are affected directly by the labor market, and in a variety of ways. Some very large corporations are vulnerable to strikes by relatively large unionized labor forces, which could cause significant losses. Thus, a change in the labor markets for such companies could affect and change the forecast for profits in the future. Like most indicators, employment statistics have to be reviewed as part of a trend.

Several employment indicators are found in the economic statistical section. The initial jobless claims, unemployment rate, and number of unemployed, are the more common and most widely reported. These statistics reflect only those individuals who have applied for unemployment or who are currently on the unemployment rolls; they exclude long-term unemployed, and those whose unemployment benefits have expired.

Reporting of these statistics, among other employment-related indicators, takes the form of comparisons to prior periods:

Employment	Latest Date	Latest Data	Preceding Period	Year Ago
Initial jobless claims	Jan. 10	322,500	318,750	351,250
Unemployment rate (%)	Dec.	4.7	3.6	5.3
Unemployed (000)	Dec.	6,392	6,289	7,167

Money Supply

Statistics for the money supply show changes in the amount of currency in circulation and available through savings deposits and checking accounts. When money supply is low—a condition called tight money—it is difficult for businesses to find loans to finance operations, so interest rates rise, pushing stock prices lower. If the money supply is allowed to move too high, it results in lower interest rates but fuels inflation. Ideally, the money supply should remain stable enough to control these economic consequences, but remain flexible enough to adjust as the economy grows.

Reporting for the money supply includes the latest available dollar amount—in billions of dollars—for three separate versions of money supply called M-1, M-2, and M-3.

First, M-1, is the basic money supply, which includes currency and demand deposits in institutions—in other words, money immediately available.

The second classification is M-2, which includes M-1 plus the value of certificates of deposit and other timed savings accounts; balances in money market mutual funds; and similar short-term money market investments.

The third version is M-3, which includes the above classifications as well as repurchase agreements and other larger money market instruments. Together, the three versions of money supply are called the monetary aggregates.

Money supply is reported in billions of dollars. A typical listing looks like this:

Money Supply	**Latest**	**Previous**	**Year Ago**
Month ended Dec. 1997:			
M1 (seasonally adjusted)	1068.5	1064.0	1076.9
M2 (seasonally adjusted)	4020.6	3997.8	3825.6
M3 (seasonally adjusted)	5334.2	5285.1	4894.4

Interest Rates

The analysis of various interest rates is of great interest to stock market investors. There is the constant concern that higher interest rates translate to lower corporate profits (thus, to less profit potential in the market). There also is a concern that investors will be attracted to higher interest rates in debt investments, and that money will then flow out of the stock market and into other areas. Less money weakens demand, so ultimately, such a move results in lower stock prices.

In studying interest rates, be aware of the constant competition for investor funds between equity investments or debt investments. Buying shares of stock directly or through mutual funds is the best known form of equity investment. When investors purchase bonds, they are lending their money to the issuers in exchange for interest. When investors place funds in savings accounts, certificates of deposit, and demand deposits, they are agreeing to allow an institution to use their funds in exchange for payment of interest. All of these are debt investments.

The analysis of interest rates includes a study of the money market, as well as rates on mortgages. In addition to showing rates for widely

---

✒ KEY POINT

Trends in interest rates are of critical importance because the stock market competes with the bond market for finite investor dollars. When bonds look more attractive than stocks because of changing interest rates, that is seen as bad news for the stock market.

---

used money market instruments, the report also includes the latest information on the three most significant measures of interest: the discount rate, the prime rate, and the federal funds rate. Reporting format for the status of rates shows the latest reported periods compared to the period immediately preceding and the same period one year ago:

Money Rates	Latest Week	Previous Week	Year Ago
Discount Rate	5	5	5
Prime Rate	8½	8½	8¼
Federal Funds Rate			
Avg. effective offer	5⅝	5⅞₆	5³⁄₁₆
Avg. weekly auction	5.74	5.45	5.28
Foreign Prime Rates			
Canada	6.00	6.00	4.75
Germany	3.55	3.59	3.11
Japan	1.625	1.625	1.625
Switzerland	3.25	2.875	3.375
Britain	7.25	7.25	6.00
T-Bill Rate			
13 weeks, Coupon Yield	5.098	5.254	5.18
13 weeks, Avg. Disc.	4.965	5.115	5.04
26 weeks, Coupon Yield	5.104	5.339	5.32
26 weeks, Avg. Disc.	4.910	5.130	5.11
52 weeks, Coupon Yield	5.341	5.341	5.61
52 weeks, Avg. Disc.	5.065	5.065	5.31
Avg. weekly auction	5.04	5.24	5.03
Broker Call Rate	7¼	7¼	7

Money Rates	Latest Week	Previous Week	Year Ago
CD Rate			
3 months	5.21	5.23	4.96
6 months	5.51	5.54	5.18
Commercial Paper Rate			
Dealer-placed			
1 month	5.45	5.51	5.42
2 months	5.44	5.51	5.43
3 months	5.42	5.48	5.44
Directly placed			
30 to 59 days	5.46	5.45	5.28
190 to 270 days	5.28	5.28	5.38
Bankers Acceptances			
1 month	5.41	5.41	5.28
2 months	5.41	5.41	5.28
3 months	5.38	5.41	5.29
6 months	5.31	5.39	5.33
Other Money Rates			
Freddie Mac Home Loan			
30-year Fixed Convertible	7.02	6.88	8.02
1-year Adjustable Mortgage	5.625	5.625	5.875
Fannie Mae Home Loan			
30-year Fixed Convertible	6.99	6.87	7.95
1-year Adjustable Mortgage	6.35	6.25	6.65
Bank Money Market	2.54	2.54	2.60
Interest Checking	1.23	1.24	1.34
6-Month Certificates	4.71	4.76	4.66
12-Month Certificates	4.97	5.02	4.93
30-Month Accounts	5.12	5.21	5.14
5-Year Certificates	5.29	5.39	5.40
U.S. Savings EE Bonds:			
Long Term (5 yrs +)	5.59	5.59	5.53

The mortgage tables show the indexes used by lenders for determining the effective rate on adjustable rate mortgages. When such loans are granted, periodic adjustments to the rate being charged are based on changes in one of the indexes reported in this section. The report appears like this:

Adjustable Mortgage Base Rates	Latest Week	Preceding Week	Year Ago
1-Year Treasury Bills	5.25	5.52	5.61
2-Year Treasury Notes	5.35	5.66	5.99
3-Year Treasury Notes	5.37	5.66	6.15
5-Year Treasury Notes	5.38	5.71	6.33
10-Year Treasury Notes	5.49	5.75	6.57
30-Year Treasury Bonds	5.75	5.93	6.80
11th District %	4.949	4.949	4.835
FHFB Contract Rate	7.34	7.34	7.55
SAIF Cost of Funds	4.93	4.98	4.76

Reports are also provided for sample yields on money market accounts and certificates of deposit of various holding duration, for various institutions around the country.

National Debt

Statistics for the current status and change in the federal debt, surplus, trade deficit, and other statistics are reported in billions of dollars, in this format:

American Debt and Deficits	Latest Report	Preceding Report	Year Ago Report
Budget Surplus/Deficit	–17.35	–35.96	–37.89
Trade Deficit	9.69	11.23	8.01
Treasury Gross Public Debt	5,486.7	5,486.3	5,311.8

Business and Economic Measurements

Overall economic information has much to do with the stock market, because the economy directly affects every listed company's future profits. Of equal interest to stock market investors is the overall business information found in the indicators. Economic statistics are reported in a variety of ways. Economic growth—durable goods produced, gross domestic product, and industrial output, for example—are reported against an index, so that the report shows a percentage increase or decrease. Other forms of growth, such as personal income or fixed investments, are reported in dollar amounts. Some factors are reported in the number of units, such as domestic autos sold.

The major economic information is compiled and reported in the form of leading economic indicators. There are 11 indicators: average monthly hours of production, average weekly initial claims for state unemployment insurance, manufacturers' new orders for consumer goods and raw materials, vendor performance, contracts for plant and equipment, new private housing permits, changes in manufacturing and trade inventory levels, changes in sensitive materials prices, stock prices, the money supply, and an index of consumer expectations.

The 11 leading economic indicators provide a broad view of trends in the economy, and they also foretell changes in other indicators. For example, checking new housing permits anticipates housing sales a few months away; changes in inventory levels anticipates future manufacturing and sales activity.

✎ KEY POINT

The leading economic indicators are valuable because they anticipate changes in growth, economic mood and direction, and the stock market.

Another grouping is referred to as lagging economic indicators. The Department of Commerce publishes a listing including seven key lagging economic indicators: average duration of unemployment, ratio of manufacturing and trade inventories to sales, changes in the index of labor costs per unit of output, average prime rate charged by banks, commercial and industrial loans outstanding, ratio of consumer installment credit outstanding, and the change in CPI for services.

The seven lagging economic indicators do not provide much in the way of information you can use to predict the mood of the stock market. However, economists and analysts see the lagging indicators as a means for confirming trends indicated in the leading indicators.

In the financial press, comparative reports for these indicators and related economic results are reported in comparative form, with the latest outcomes compared to the preceding ones and to the same outcomes one year before.

🗝 *KEY POINT*

Lagging economic indicators are not directly useful for stock market analysis, but they are used to confirm what the leading economic indicators reveal.

Stock Market and Investor Sentiment

Economic indicators also summarize activity in the stock market, showing New York Stock Exchange volume in the number of stock shares and bond dollar volume traded; number of securities sold; and the total value of listed stocks.

Sentiment of investors is an intangible. You are trying to measure how investors feel about the market, the economy, or a specific company. However, a trend watcher can judge the mood of the market by surveying sentiment in a number of ways. *Barron's* weekly report estimates investor sentiment by showing percentage of bulls versus bears as measured by several different sources.

Putting Indicators to Work

Economic indicators, to many investors, are not as interesting as the financial results of one company. Those results have an obvious and direct affect on the stock's market price. Thus, it is easy to see the cause and effect, whereas national economic indicators and their affect are not as readily apparent.

As one of many tests you can apply in your program for fundamental analysis, a study of key indicators can provide you with a good forecasting tool. If the industry in which your stocks are active is particularly sensitive to interest rates, employment, and the money supply, then national trends will have a very serious impact on those stocks.

As a starting point, your analysis of a company as an investment candidate should include the gaining of a thorough understanding of the industry as a whole and that company's place in the industry. Consider the four following questions:

1. *What is the primary activity in the industry?* Be sure you know exactly what industry your company is in, and what takes place

within that industry. This requires research. For example, a soup company is not necessarily involved only in selling soup. They might own many subsidiary companies and have diversified into more than one line of business. If the company you are watching and thinking of investing in has a primary activity representing the majority of its sales, you should be sure you know exactly what that industry involves, and what types of sales are included. The same information is important if you already own stock and want to monitor for changes that threaten potential future growth.

2. *What outside economic factors influence profits and operations?* Each industry can be defined and distinguished not only by what it sells and produces, but also by the types of risks to which its members are sensitive. In a labor-intensive manufacturing business, employment trends will have a lot to do with future profits. A company competing with international companies will be vulnerable to fluctuating currency exchange rates, inflation here and abroad, and political as well as economic indicators.

3. *What forms of diversification by the company mitigate outside influences?* Does a company become involved in several dissimilar industries, or does it stay with one primary product or service line? Diversification helps a company overcome the potential problems in single economic indicators. Obviously risks can never be eliminated completely, but they can be mitigated through diversification. This could be used as a test for determining whether to place a company's stock on your list of likely investments.

4. *How can you diversify your portfolio to protect against economic risk?* As a stock market investor, you probably will not want to invest exclusively in one industry, any more than you would invest all of your capital in one company's stock. Diversification is a sound investment management decision and—like the corporations you consider for investment—sound management over your portfolio is essential. Be aware of a company's exposure to economic risk and seek ways to invest in different industries whose economic risks are not identical.

CHAPTER 12

Different Drummer Investing *or* The March of the Contrarians

"I am a lone, lorn creetur ... and everythink goes contrairy with me."
Charles Dickens, *David Copperfield*

So might any investor say when following the fundamentals, considering the greater appeal of technical analysis. In the market, as anywhere else, it takes self-confidence and a belief in the right method to break with the crowd, to think for yourself, and to ignore the mentality of the herd.

You need to remind yourself—constantly—about some market realities:

- The crowd usually is wrong.
- Professional analysts and managers are usually wrong.
- By the time everyone agrees on something, its time has passed.

These are, indeed, contrary points of view. To believe in the minority is intimidating, because it requires independent thought, belief, and faith. It is always easier to go along with the majority point of view, where one is not required to support a belief system. There is comfort in conformity.

Contrarians believe that comfort comes at the price of being wrong. Because the majority is more often wrong than right about market direction, timing, and trends, the majority of investors can easily fall into the trap of being wrong. It is the easy way. To develop a plan and have faith in it, as well as the confidence to be guided by what makes sense, is the way to succeed in the market, but it is not the easy way nor the popular way.

The Contrarian as Fundamentalist

Is being a contrarian the same as being a fundamentalist? Not necessarily. When you consider the investment strategy of the market in general, you find that technical analysis is far more popular. The Dow Jones Industrial Average, the major indicator and for many the market itself, has nothing to do with fundamentals. Chart watching and attention to other nonfinancial indexes makes the majority of individual investors technicians. So in the sense of comparisons to the market, you will be contrarian if you trust fundamentals as a primary means of information.

✦ KEY POINT

If you believe in *and* act on fundamental information, you are a contrarian.

The contrarian theory is not the same as a comparison between technical and fundamental schools of thought, however. As a broad definition, contrarians believe that it is the nature of group thinking to miss the point and to guess wrong. A contrarian has observed that real market opportunities occur by not agreeing with the current trend. Specifically, if there is a sudden drop in prices accompanied by a panic, the contrarian remains cool and looks for buying opportunities. On the other side, when a sudden run-up in the market or a specific stock causes a buying stampede, the contrarian recognizes the vulnerability of the situation and quietly sells at a profit or sits back and waits for things to settle down.

This is fundamentalist thinking in that it is long-term rather than short-term. The day-to-day trading strategies are seen as passing matters of relatively little importance over time. The fundamentalist uses current information only to look for signals that a hold should be changed to a sell position, rather than to buy and/or sell actively.

As a fundamentalist, you also recognize the nature of crowd thinking. Crowds often are wrong and, whether right or wrong, they think not with their individual minds but with a mindless and illogical method that cannot be given responsibility, only blind authority. The market as a whole acts at times like entire communities caught up in a particular idea. A study of human nature in history reveals this tendency. Historian Charles Mackay observed this by stating:

> We find that whole communities suddenly fix their minds upon one object, and go mad in its pursuit; that millions of people become simultaneously impressed with one delusion, and run after it, till their attention is caught by some new folly more captivating than the first.

Mackay aptly describes the stock market mindset and the nature of investing in general. At various times, sudden hysteria in the stock market, real estate, gold, and other investments has seized populations and inspired reckless actions, often to the point that people's lives have been ruined. Remember that by its nature, a mass of people cannot be expected to think logically and clearly, especially when under pressure because situations have changed suddenly.

🔑 KEY POINT

There is great danger in going along with the majority. History shows that group thinking often is wrong, sometimes drastically wrong.

The fundamentalist is coldly scientific and—while perhaps having less fun or excitement than the technician—tends to think of the market and the cause and effect of investment value in a scientific manner. This is a contrary point of view to the usual way of thinking about the market. You are unlikely to find a more suspicious group of people than stockbrokers and traders. The contrary approach of fundamental analysis is best seen in the comparison between actions and perceptions. Most technicians, when asked, will swear by the fundamentals. They will agree that the answers are all in the financial numbers and that, when all is said and done, the numbers are the whole story. However, they will then look to the patterns of charts and spend many hours speculating about the direction of the DJIA in the next six months. Thus, even the dedicated technician will say that he or she believes in the fundamentals, but would rather spend time trying to forecast the indexes than study a financial statement.

The scientific mind of the fundamental analyst is what makes the difference. It is the belief in the fundamentals accompanied by the practice of decision making based on the same information that defines the real fundamentalist. In this sense, it is contrary to stay on course and to not be led astray into speculation about the Dow—that is, you refuse to make decisions on the basis of pure guesswork. This is the flaw in most market thinking. It is very easy for anyone, including professionals, to profess belief in the fundamentals but to end up acting on nonfundamental information.

Is this a problem only for individual investors? Not at all. Professional managers and analysts are perhaps more susceptible to distracted thinking and crowd mentality than individuals, because they exist in the market environment; that is their job. You should listen closely to stockbrokers, financial planners, and analysts. They might have many good ideas based on fundamentals, but what is the decision-making criterion? Does the professional suggest taking actions now based on movement in the Dow? Do they depend on chart patterns to time buy and sell decisions? Do they ultimately abandon the fundamentals after the analysis, and make their decisions or recommendations for other reasons?

If you make use of professional services—stockbrokers or financial planners, for example—pay close attention to their sources for recommendations. Be wary when advice is given to you solely on the basis of technical indicators. As easy as it is to use such highly available and visual indicators as the DJIA, these indicators are not reliable for the purpose of making long-term decisions in your portfolio. Perhaps the greatest problem in asking for advice from others is that you cannot always identify why they recommend a particular course, what purpose is being served, or what types of information have been replied on to arrive at the conclusion.

Just as you need to always remember the nature of crowds and their tendency to be wrong, it does not mean that the general attitude is always wrong. You can take contrary thinking too far by completely rejecting all market wisdom and acting contrary to all information you receive. This would not be logical. The contrarian does not reject all information, but tends to be highly selective and to think like an individual rather than as part of the larger market.

> 🔑 *KEY POINT*
>
> Listen carefully when others give you market advice. What is the source of their reasoning?

Why Contrary Theory Works

Observant market watchers have seen repeated confirmation of the theory that the mass of the market is usually wrong—not just the amateur investor, but the majority of professionals as well. You may recall that a previously cited 1985 study by *Consumer Reports* revealed that only 63 of 289 stock mutual funds outperformed the Standard & Poor's (S&P) 500 over a five-year period.[*] These funds are professionally managed; yet, less than 22 percent did better than the broad-based S&P 500.

Do not fall for the illusion that professionals perform in the market any better than you can. In fact, one of the highly successful market stories is the history of investment clubs, a form of small, informally managed mutual investing. A small group of people, usually under 20, pool their funds and invest together. If these groups follow fundamental principles, history has shown, investment clubs tend to profit significantly better than market averages. This information, compared to the mutual fund study, could indicate that mutual fund managers might tend to be distracted by technical indicators and crowd thinking; and that adherence to formula investing based on fundamental decision making is the right way to go.

> 🔑 *KEY POINT*
>
> Statistics show that you may do better investing without professional help than you will do depending on someone else. Some distance from the daily workings of the market might be a plus.

---

[*] *Consumer Reports*, 1985 (A more recent survey by Morningstar, Inc., studied the same question for United States diversified stock funds. Those beating the S&P 500 were down to a dismal 10 percent in 1997—cited in *The New York Times*, January 11, 1998.)

Investment clubs following the strategic approach recommended by the organization for such clubs, the National Association of Investment Clubs (NAIC), will very likely do well in the market. (For more information, contact the NAIC at 711 West Thirteen Mile Road, Madison Heights, MI 48071; telephone, 810-583-3212; fax, 810-583-4880.) The NAIC suggests four principles: (1) invest regularly, regardless of the market outlook; (2) reinvest all earnings; (3) invest in growth companies; and (4) diversify to reduce risk.* The advantage an investment club has is twofold. First, the organization is small enough so that each member can have direct and significant impact on the investment policies and strategies of the club; and if any members are tempted to stray from the fundamental approach, other members will tend to redirect that member. Second, the organization is small enough to manage effectively and to make decisions in a timely manner—which might not be true for mutual funds, which handle millions of dollars in investment assets.

The investment club approach, like individual methods of fundamental analysis, is largely contrarian because it assumes a long-term point of view and intentionally ignores the momentary news of the market. This is especially true regarding price movement and DJIA levels. One market test used by contrarians is the odd lot theory. This is an approach based on the belief that odd lot traders are usually wrong, and that a significant change in trading patterns should be taken as a reverse signal.

An odd lot is a trade of fewer than 100 shares of stock. In order to minimize trading costs, stock is normally traded in round lots of 100 shares or shares traded in multiples of 100. By trading in round lots, commission costs are standardized. You may trade in odd lots, but you will pay a higher commission for the privilege. As a general rule, odd lot traders are people who do not wish to purchase 100 shares of stock. Generally speaking, such a trader cannot afford to buy a full round lot; thus, the odd lot trader tends to be a novice with limited capital. Followers of this theory believe that when the volume of odd lot trading grows substantially, it serves as a signal to take the opposite action—a purely contrarian approach.

---

* Thomas O. O'Hara and Kenneth S. Janke, Sr., *Starting and Running a Profitable Investment Club*, Times Business, 1996, p. 16.

The odd lot theory is called a sentiment indicator because it measures what investors are thinking, rather than some financial or index movement or value. Economists like to measure what consumers think as a means for determining the direction of the economy; likewise, market watchers believe that future market movements can be predicted by measuring what investors think. However, the contrarian does not put faith in the opinions of odd lot traders; rather, they believe that more than any other trader, the odd lot trader is invariably wrong, and the opposite action is indicated. So when buying volume among odd lot traders grows, that should signal selling activity; and when selling among odd lot traders grows, that should signal buying activity.

Like so many nonfundamental theories, the odd lot theory is broadly generalized and even biased. After all, if you assume that odd lot buyers do not make the right decisions, then why should you invest based on indicators they develop? Even though the odd lot theory tells you to do everything in opposite, that does not mean that the odd lot theory should be used dependably and exclusively. As with all forms of market information, the odd lot theory is one among many indicators and should be used along with other information. As a general rule, any indicated change in the market should be confirmed by other tests before you act.

Example: You are considering investing proceeds from the sale of an investment property in common stocks. You have been watching several growth companies lately, and you are looking for key indicators as to whether or not the timing makes sense. The odd lot statistics show a recent large run-up in buy volume. Under the odd lot theory, this should signal that now is not the time to buy. However, you don't want to act on this information alone. You will depend on other indicators, specifically the fundamentals of the specific companies in which you plan to invest, as well as trends in the industries involved. You plan to monitor net margin, sales volume, price-earnings (PE) ratio, earnings per share, dividend yield, and other tests, not just the odd lot information.

In this example, the odd lot activity may be troubling because, if you accept the theory, it could be bad timing to purchase stocks at this moment. This often is as far as investors go—finding a theory that is relatively easy to monitor and then depending on that theory as the sole means for decision making. It makes more sense to use theories like the odd lot theory as a means for performing other tests or exer-

> ### ☝ *KEY POINT*
>
> A single indicator that catches your attention might give you insight to the market, but any single indicator should be confirmed before you act.

cising greater caution, but ultimately acting based on what the fundamentals reveal.

In this instance, you might discover that a flattening in sales activity and a rising PE ratio indicate that stocks are overpriced, and that waiting until prices and the trends settle down makes sense. Alternatively, you might conclude that the fundamentals look better than ever and the odd lot indicator is too generalized and doesn't seem to apply. Thus you will not wait, but will act now on the fundamental information you have compiled.

Odd lot information is market-wide for the most part, so watching this statistic might give you only market-wide opinion. This is relatively meaningless when you are thinking of purchasing a specific stock. In many cases, a momentary mood or trend in the market has no effect whatsoever on one stock's value. At any rate, the concern and the deciding factors should be long-term in nature. The odd lot theory is a favorite contrarian indicator, and can help in the timing of purchases and sales; it should not serve as your sole means of analysis.

Viewing the Larger Market Picture

The major difference between fundamental and technical thinking is based on a contrary attitude. Technicians tend to interpret signs—chart patterns and the DJIA are primary examples—and to conclude something about the market from those signs. As a consequence, technicians tend to react as a group and to ignore underlying fundamental information, even when that information is clear. In a sense, technicians are the conformists of the market. They are the voice of the herd.

This is why the majority of professionals are wrong most of the time. They look for signals that have several attributes. First, the signals must be easily and quickly found. Second, they must be clear as to their meaning. And third, the signals must be universally understood by the

🐿 *KEY POINT*

Professionals tend to look for signals that can be found quickly and easily, that have a clear meaning, and that are understood by everyone. Unfortunately, these signals often are lacking in any real value.

technicians. There is only one thing missing in this list of requirements: The signals must have some relevance to value and direction of the market.

The fundamentalist, in comparison, is truly contrarian. Not depending on price patterns or the Dow Jones Industrial Average, the fundamentalist who adheres to the fundamental rules will tend to identify trend patterns, to think independently, and to look for exceptional information rather than formula indicators.

In the sense of how information is reviewed, the fundamentalist recognizes that there are no clear, easy signals that everyone will interpret in the same manner. There are no secrets. There are no magic formulas that will provide insight into what is about to happen. The market is preoccupied with trying to outguess the other investors, to get insight on some change before everyone else. How does the fundamentalist use information to succeed in the long term?

The answer is not so much in interpretation of any single fundamental trend. It is with the creative combination of trends that the fundamentalist ultimately outperforms the market and the typical professional. You may set a rule for yourself that you will never act on a solitary source of information, that you will always act on confirmation of trends in two or more dependable indicators.

Example: You may use a combination of six different fundamental and technimental indicators. These may include sales volume, net margin, debt/equity ratio, PE ratio, net earnings per share, and volatility. All of these tests are performed as part of a trend and never alone. You also like to watch the odd lot statistics and overall market volume as a means for keeping an eye on general mood of the market. Your rules include the following standards:

- No decisions are made without being confirmed in at least three of the trends.

- No hold decision will be reversed until a trend is firmly established in a majority of the indicators being monitored, recognizing that such a change is a departure from the long-term strategy.
- No buy decision is made for new investments without a stock first being qualified in all of the indicators you watch.

Such a range of generalized rules is valuable because it places structure in your portfolio, and enables you to develop your own signals. You will discover that risk of market loss is dramatically reduced when you apply a series of sensible rules, consistently and over time. Be a contrarian in the very methods you use to develop a risk management strategy. Don't accept the general ideas offered by others if you believe that the combined approach you develop for yourself makes more sense.

🔑 KEY POINT

Setting investment rules for yourself is necessary and smart. Without rules, how do you know how to react to changing conditions?

Also become an avid financial statement watcher. You don't have to become an accountant to comprehend the essence of what is occurring within a company. You will see gradual changes and trends as they emerge over time if you study financial reports and track the fundamentals.

Most importantly, never invest in a new company, or sell a stock you currently hold, solely on rumor or the suggestion of another person. The stock market operates on the fuel of rumor and is generally lacking in a clear direction. The auction marketplace enables a large number of people and institutions to trade efficiently, and it provides a ready market on a daily basis. But it does not offer you order or logic. Because the market operates purely on a momentary supply and demand force, there is no time for careful analysis; the daily decisions about buy, hold, and sell, and about how and why prices change, are made purely in response to ever-changing perceptions. The news and rumors floating around at any one time about a company, an industry, changes in the DJIA, politics, the economy, and other influences, are never ending. You will learn to take refuge in the fundamentals, simply by observing the irrationality of the market. The greatest danger of participating in the market is that you will become attracted to the excitement of short-term profits, speculation, and wild rumor; and that you will find more satisfaction in the frenzy than in long-term profits.

If this occurs, you may protect your capital by segmenting it. Keep the majority in long-term investments and operate on the fundamental. Take a relatively small portion to use for speculation. Try this for a year, and see which approach yields the greatest profits. Try it for two years, or for five years, and test the two approaches again. You can be sure that in the long run, the fundamental approach will be the more profitable one. A short-term spectacular return on a high-risk strategy is difficult to repeat, whereas fundamental long-term investing does work over the years.

⚓ KEY POINT

The best way to test long-term fundamental investing against short-term speculation is to try both. But use only a small part of your total capital when you speculate, because you probably will lose it.

Contrary thinking can be used for short-term speculative gains, although this is not the same range of techniques as those used by fundamentalists. For example, if you keep a small portion of your portfolio available for speculation, you may act on contrary signals.

Example: The DJIA falls by several hundred points. Many volatile stocks lose 10 points or more. This presents a short-term buying opportunity because as the market corrects from the overreaction seen in the DJIA, those stocks will tend to recover their price loss. Remember, the key advantage here grows from a tendency toward short-term overreaction in the market as a whole.

Example: A rumor begins concerning a company's major product, involving possible litigation or government intervention. If this rumor is true, the company stands to lose money. As a consequence, the stock falls by 35 percent. Again, this presents a short-term speculative opportunity. The market overreacts, so even with bad news, the degree of reaction is usually excessive. While you stand the risk of the rumor being true and the stock falling even more, perhaps even total failure of the corporation, chances are that in the short term, the immediate stock price change will reverse itself, at least to some degree.

Example: A company's stock price is rising rapidly on positive news, and investors are making big profits. However, you observe that the PE ratio is outpacing the news, and that profits are not increasing dramatically. The higher PE ratio is a danger signal when the change occurs in the short term, an indication that the stock's market price is inflated beyond reasonable levels. This may be taken as a short-term sell signal.

Notice that in all of these examples, the contrarian point of view is short term and seems to be high-risk in nature. You buy at a time when the stock's value seems most questionable; you sell when the price is climbing rapidly. It is absolutely contrary to the fever of the market as a whole; the risks are high because the action is speculative. You stand to make big profits, avoid sudden losses, and beat the market. You also stand to suffer big losses, miss out on profits, and end up losing a lot of money while the market as a whole steers clear of the risk. Such is the nature of speculation.

As you can see, contrarians can take the form of long-term fundamental investors, or short-term, high-risk speculators. In either case, the strategy makes much more sense than the more common approach, going along with what most people think. There is greater risk in following what others are doing than there is in thinking for yourself and acting against the trend.

Risks for Contrarians

At first glance, it might seem that simply acting in a contrary mode is itself a risk. In some respects, it is; going against the thinking of the majority might be thought of as a form of reassurance risk. Allowing a majority to dictate decision making is very reassuring, but it takes more strength to make individual decisions that most people dispute. The fact is, going along with the majority is a much greater risk, in virtually every way.

✦ KEY POINT

The big risk is not in striking out on your own and going against the majority; the real risk is taking the easy way and following majority thinking.

Other risks have to be kept in mind and, as a fundamentalist, you need to make specific policy decisions about how to manage the various risks. As a contrarian, you might reject the popular thinking about risk, especially if you have ultimate faith in fundamental analysis and, at the same time, you decide to defy the traditional thinking about risks.

First is the concept of diversification. The general opinion about smart investment management states that you should never invest all of your capital in one place; rather, you should spread it around so that you never stand to lose everything on one change. Diversification can mean several different things. It may mean that within the stock market, you should not buy just one stock. Or you should not put all of your capital in the stock of a single industry. Or you should diversify between equity and debt investments. Or you should have some portion in domestic and some in international stocks. Or you should have some of your portfolio in real estate or precious metals.

However you define diversification, it means spreading your exposure to risk among many dissimilar investments. So as a contrarian, do you accept this premise? This is one of the areas in which it generally seems to make sense to go along with the broad thinking, that it makes sense to spread risks. In practice, you may be acting as a contrarian to follow the advice, especially when you look at how most individual investors act. They may have too much of their capital invested in a single stock or, equally as dangerous, in a single strategy. Thus, if the market goes opposite of the way they think, they will lose from lack of diversification in strategy. Many investors subscribe to the theory of diversification but fail to put it into practice.

If you have limited capital, you can diversify by investing in mutual funds rather than buying your own stocks directly. The cost is lower and diversification is automatic, although you place your trust in the fund's management rather than doing your own analysis. Your investment decision is limited to the selection of a mutual fund, but you have no say in the decision of which investments to buy. Many motivated

> ### ⨞ KEY POINT
>
> Contrarians don't ignore the importance of diversification. Smart contrarians *really* practice it and don't just talk about the concept.

investors prefer to sacrifice diversification in exchange for having more control in managing their own portfolios.

Great emphasis is placed on market risk, which of course means the risk that the price of stock will fall. This is usually a form of short-term risk and, as you have already seen, short-term investment strategies can be used speculatively or even for the timing of long-term decisions. However, we suggest a contrarian point of view for fundamentalists: Ignore the short-term market risk. Make investment decisions using the dependable fundamentals, using and applying a long-term point of view about a company's investment value. Ignore the day-to-day changes in price insofar as they affect decision making, and track stock price movement only as a matter of vested interest. One of the satisfying things about investing in the stock market is price watching, especially if you are not likely to change a long-term strategy based on a day's price movement.

So you may ignore market risk as it applies in short-term changes, recognizing that the real value of your investment is its worth many years from now, the reward for well-researched selections of growth stocks.

Let's segment market risk into two parts. The more popularly understood is the short-term changes in market price. The other longer-term growth-oriented risk is of greater concern to the fundamentalist. Remember, the market rewards investors for taking risks; otherwise, there would be no interest in the stock market. Equity investors make money if they hold onto growth stocks for many years. As company profits grow, so does the equity value of the investment. With this in mind, the daily fluctuations in market price have no immediate interest because it means nothing in long-term fundamental terms.

Knowing which risks to follow and which ones to ignore is the best method for limiting your exposure to risk. In some respects, fundamentalists do not suffer from market risk in the same way as speculators do because they are not interested in immediate price movement. Speculators are highly vulnerable to immediate market risk because

🏃 KEY POINT

Market risk can be ignored to the extent that it represents a short-term risk. Your concern should be for long-term growth prospects rather than day-to-day price changes.

they intentionally expose themselves to high risk as a means for seeking high, short-term profits. But there are important differences. If you pick stocks using fundamental analysis, you will earn profits over time, just by applying sound ideas consistently. However, speculators are assured with equal certainty that they will ultimately lose money. That is true because of the nature of high risk. Speculators eventually lose because it is increasingly difficult to always make a large profit. They are constantly exposed to high risk and cannot consistently beat the odds.

CHAPTER 13

Fundamentals in Specialized Markets

*T*he application of fundamental analysis works in all investment markets, not just the stock market. The lessons of the fundamentals can be applied elsewhere, although the attributes of the stock market contain some features not always available in other markets:

- Published, independently audited financial statements
- A ready market for all buyers and sellers
- Effective and broad regulation over market practices and disclosures
- Readily available information for the public
- A high degree of liquidity

Most other markets lack one or more of these attributes, making stock market investing not only convenient, but also relatively safe. For example, you can normally depend on the accuracy and completeness of financial statements published about publicly listed companies, because they have been put through independent audits, and because publicly listed companies and their records must meet the mandates of the Securities and Exchange Commission.

Distinctions between Stocks

One of the important points often missed, even by long-time stock market investors, is the fairly obvious point that risks vary among different stocks. Investors like to talk about varying degrees of volatility, changing price-earnings (PE) ratios, positive or negative news, and changes in fundamental indicators, not to mention the ever-changing market prices. However, even with all of that information out there and available, investors often fail in the logical next step of quantifying the information in terms of risk.

🔑 KEY POINT

You should always keep in mind the risk factors involved with various indicators, and how risk factors match your personal perceptions about how much risk is appropriate.

The question that everyone should be asking—fundamentalists and technicians alike—is: What defines a "safe" stock investment and what defines a "risky" stock investment? Each investor must answer the following four questions:

1. What is your individual definition of risk? In other words, how do you define your own risk tolerance level?
2. What type of risk is being discussed?
3. Is the risk immediate or long-term in nature?
4. What is the relative risk? That is to say, in a review of several alternatives, is one choice more or less risky than the others? (This question is critical because some investors naturally are attracted to high risks; thus, it would be unfair to characterize an investment selection as too risky if, in fact, it fits an investor's preferences.)

Surprisingly, many astute investors fail to define and assess the risks of the investments they select. Even the most analytical fundamentalist might become overly concerned with the numerical values and trends found in financial information, ignoring the inherent volatility of a stock; the quality of the company's management team; and perhaps, a loss of market within the industry as other companies begin to emerge as new leaders. These indicators—fundamental, readily available, and important in the analysis—relate to definitions of risk, notably to long-term risk.

A safe stock must meet your definition of acceptable risk—market risk as well as other forms. Most fundamentalists seek long-term growth prospects, so that it becomes necessary to look beyond the historical fundamentals. You may be interested in determining that a company has the potential to remain an industry leader or, if not currently the leader, to move into a leading position in the future.

Below we will discuss the three methods for identifying the degree of risk among different stocks volatility, rapidly growing PE ratio, and capital strength or weakness.

Volatility. Perhaps the most immediate sign of market risk is volatility, the tendency for a stock's price to change in a recent period of time. By testing beta, or keeping an eye on the volatility of the price of a stock, you can identify the short-term tendency of the company.

Placing a relative value on volatility is only the first step. It is a means for defining market risk according to the recent price history of a stock. While it is technical rather than fundamental information, it can serve as a means for further investigation. Why is a particular stock volatile, in comparison with other stocks? The answer might be related to recent gossip or rumor, to a market perception about the company, or to other outside influences or news. Or the answer might be found in the fundamentals. An examination of financial statements might reveal historical trends that themselves have been volatile: inconsistent growth patterns in sales, widely ranging profit and loss outcomes, large one-time adjustments in valuation or write-off history of subsidiary losses; activity in mergers, acquisitions, and divestitures; changing dividend payment policies, frequent changes in top management, labor problems, and product liability; and numerous other possible matters of significance, any of which might affect the fundamentals.

Such information points to potential problems in long-term growth as well. Is the fundamental volatility a growing pain, or does

✺ KEY POINT

Volatility itself does not necessarily tell you what you need to know about risk. High volatility can lead you to examine the root causes, which is fundamentally more interesting and more revealing.

it characterize the company, the industry, management, or accounting practices of the company? Further investigation is warranted when you find that volatile fundamentals underlie volatile price history.

Rapidly growing PE ratio. Market risk will also appear in the form of rapidly growing PE ratios. Remember that the PE ratio is a comparison between market price and earnings, so if the PE expands quickly, it is a sign that the market perception about potential future earnings has improved in the short term. This can be translated into greater risk that the perception is wrong, and that the price will suffer a correction in the future. It can also mean that the stock will continue to rise in price and those who invest now will profit in the short term. There is no way to tell with consistency what outcome will occur in the future.

🔑 KEY POINT

A rapidly climbing PE ratio means that market perception about market price potential is outpacing profits—a sign that you may want to look cautiously at whether the fundamentals support that perception.

Capital strength or weakness. Fundamentals generally measure one trend or the trend in related financial outcomes. However, overall capital strength as a long-term fundamental indicator is found in the tests of several ratios: capitalization ratio, return on equity, or tests of working capital, for example. In terms of risk, it is not the amount of capital that should be evaluated exclusively, but also the source (equity of debt capitalization), the effect of capital sources on profits (comparative trends in interest and profits), and the ability of the corporation to continue expanding. The idea of capital strength is a judgment about effective management as much as one of financial results from one year to the next.

🔑 KEY POINT

The test of capital strength tells you about management quality and not just about the numbers.

Fundamentals in the Bond Market

Besides observing fundamentals and their place in stock market portfolio management, you can see how financial information works in the bond market. While bond market investors have a different approach than those in the stock market, they still need to observe a company's fundamentals as part of their decision making.

A bond investor is not interested in a company's growth potential. However, its capital strength and credit rating are of paramount importance, because bond investors want to be assured that the company will be able to repay the bond amount. A bond investor does not care about whether a company earns a profit, dominates its industry, or acquires other companies. The only immediate concern is the safety of the debt and the company's ability to repay.

In the bond market, it is not profit or profitability that matters, but credit rating. Standard & Poor's and other companies rate corporate debt according to the company's financial strength and ability to repay. Every company depending on debt financing wants the highest possible debt rating, because higher ratings translate to lower interest expense. That's because safer debt investments are more desirable. The highest Standard & Poor's long-term credit rating is AAA. This means that in the opinion of the rating company, the corporation has an extremely strong capacity to meet its obligations. Three other grades reflect gradually diminishing quality from AA (very strong) to A (strong) to BBB (adequate). The top four ratings are considered investment grade bonds.

When the rating service assigns a BB, B, CCC, CC, or C to bonds, they are considered to be increasingly speculative. Bonds in these classifications have been collectively referred to as junk bonds. One final classification worth noting assigned by Standard & Poor's is D, which means the company is in payment default.

Investors are also interested in the interest rate paid on a bond. Like stock market valuation, bond interest changes as the result of supply and demand. In the bond market, competition for finite debt investment capital exists not only among corporations, but also between corporate and government bond issuers. Bonds are issued to finance the national debt, states' debt and operations, and local governments and subdivisions as well.

Rate of return for bonds does not necessarily mean the nominal interest rate only (the stated annual rate of interest). For example, a bond with a nominal rate of 8 percent pays 8 percent of the par value

⚡ *KEY POINT*

Bond market value changes based on changing interest rates; bonds might be worth more or less than their par value.

of the bond. Par value, also called face value, is the amount that was originally issued and the amount that will be repaid. A bond is not always currently valued at par value, however.

The interest rate paid—the nominal interest rate—is fixed contractually for the life of the bond. However, there is no way to know whether that interest rate will be high or low relative to a current market rate in the future. This is a risk factor for bond investors. If a bond turns out to have a relatively high rate compared to future market rates, then its market value will move above market value, and it can be traded at a premium. If a bond turns out to have a relatively low rate compared to future market rates, then its market value moves below market rates. If sold, it commands a discounted value from its par value.

When a bond is valued above or below its par value, the current interest rate is different than the nominal interest rate because current market value of the bond has changed.

Example: A particular bond carries a nominal interest rate of 5 percent. However, the bond is currently trading at a discount of 97. To compute current rate, divide the nominal interest rate by the discount percentage. In this example, the current rate is 5.15 percent:

$$\frac{5}{97} = 5.15\%$$

Example: A bond carries a nominal rate of 5 percent. However, its market value is now at a premium of 102. Current rate is 4.90 percent:

$$\frac{5}{102} = 4.90\%$$

Premiums and discounts are the special features of concern to bond investors. Unlike shareholders who assume equity positions and are interested in the long-term growth prospects of their companies, bond investors are debtors. They compete with shareholders for profits.

Some portion of profits go to the payment of long-term bond interest, and the remainder is available to fund new expansion or to pay dividends. The greater the burden of interest paid to bondholders, the lower the earnings per share. Thus, bondholders and shareholders have an adversarial interest in their investment positions.

Bondholders have a contractual priority over common shareholders (but not over preferred shareholders). In the event of default, bond interest will be paid before dividends; and in the event of complete business failure, bonds are repaid before shareholders are provided any return. Thus, bondholders may have a degree of security in their position, but they will never realize the potential that long-term investors stand to have from selecting growth stocks.

The Options Market and Diversification

The relationship between fundamental analysis and risk raises the question How can you protect a profitable position or mitigate the threat of losses? In the long-term sense, the answer is that by selecting stocks based on a complete analysis of the fundamentals, such losses are mitigated drastically. In the short term, you can also use options to protect positions.

Options generally are considered to be high-risk investments. In the most popular ways they are used, they are high risk. However, two specific strategies can be used to reduce risk or to tie in profits, and should be considered as highly conservative strategies.

🏃 *KEY POINT*

Buying options is highly speculative except when used as part of a stock investment strategy. Some option strategies are highly conservative.

Here is a brief overview of the options market. An option is an intangible right, a contract that provides its buyer with privileges in exchange for a purchase; specifically, the owner of an option has a right to buy or sell 100 shares of stock at a specified price, regardless of what the current market price is for that stock. A single stock option provides this right for 100 shares of stock.* Each option has specific attributes to it:

- The option is specific to one particular stock, called the underlying stock, and provides a right for 100 shares per option contract. Every option exists and pertains only to one specific company's stock, and is not interchangeable.
- A call option gives its owner the right to purchase 100 shares of stock. A put option gives its owner the right to sell 100 shares of stock.
- The option will expire in the near future. It exists only until the expiration date. After that date, the option is worthless.
- The option has a market value, called the premium. This premium rises and falls in accordance with the difference between current market value and the strike price, which is the price per share the option buyer has locked in.

There is a lot of terminology involved with the options market, which is unfortunate because it requires quite a learning curve just to grasp the concepts, learn the rules, and apply those rules to the question of managing your own risks. Options generally are highly speculative because they exist for only a short period of time. In order to make a profit as an option buyer, you depend on a significant movement in the stock's price, which will make the option more valuable. Time works against option buyers, and it is more likely that they will lose money than that they will make a profit.

The fundamentals of the option market are vastly different from those for stocks, because options are intangible. They exist as rights to

✦ KEY POINT

Buying options is highly speculative because they expire in the near future. Time works against the option buyer.

---

* Options also are available for entire indexes, based on the New York Stock Exchange, Standard & Poor's indexes, the Value Line Index, and others. But for the purpose of explaining the use of options to reduce stock investment risk, the discussion here is limited to stock options.

take future action and do not hold any permanent value. So while an option's value is dependent entirely on near-term price changes in the stock, they lack any fundamental value except the current premium—based on supply and demand—and on the current price of the stock.

For most moderate to conservative investors, buying options as speculative devices is far beyond the risk tolerance level. However, options can serve a purpose even in the most conservative portfolio. The two conservative strategies you can use in your portfolio provide a form of short-term insurance in situations where prices have risen dramatically. They can improve profits in situations where you would sell if you could get a specific price. They are (1) buying temporary portfolio insurance and (2) creating higher profits on sale. They are discussed below.

Buying Temporary Portfolio Insurance

The first conservative strategy involves using options to ensure profits in a specific stock. Most people understand the proper use of insurance. You pay a premium to buy protection against loss. If the loss occurs, the insurer reimburses you. If the loss does not occur, the insurance premium is viewed as a cost of protection against the risk, a means for offsetting the exposure.

A put option can be used in this manner to protect a profit. A put is a contract that provides you the right to sell 100 shares of stock at a specified price by a specified expiration date. That price is unchanging, so that if the market value of stock falls below that price, the put has ensured the price level you target. Even long-term investors may run into situations in which a relatively short-term paper profit is worth protecting.

Example: You bought 100 shares of stock last year at $32 per share. The price remained in a fairly narrow trading range until last week, when it suddenly rose to $43 per share. You cannot find any immediate reason for the sudden change in price, and you suspect that the price will correct itself in the near future. You can buy a "40 put" (meaning the right to sell 100 shares of stock at $40 per share) for $200, and that put will not expire for three months.

What happens in this situation? Consider the three possibilities: the market price rises, the market price remains the same, or the market price falls.

1. *The market price rises.* If the price continues to rise between now and the option's expiration date, then you have given up

$200 for the protection of the put. You lose that $200 when the option expires. The loss can be deducted on your income tax return as a short-term capital loss. Meanwhile, the rising stock remains profitable.

2. *The market price remains the same.* The outcome is the same as above. You gain nothing from the option insurance because you lose no market value in the stock.

3. *The market price falls.* This is the situation in which the put provides price protection. Because the contract provides that you can sell 100 shares at $40 per share, the put becomes more valuable as the stock's market value falls. This does not mean you have to sell the stock. It only means that you have insurance in the event that the stock does fall. If, for example, the value of the stock fell back to $35 per share before the put's expiration, that put would increase in value point-for-point below $40 per share. So you could take one of two actions before the expiration date. First, you could exercise the option, enabling you to sell 100 shares of stock at $40 per share. In that case, your profit will be $600 (before deducting trading fees). That is a 100-share computation combining stock and option transactions:

Option exercise price of $40 per share	$ 4,000
Less: purchase price of stock, $32 per share	– 3,200
Less: option premium	– 200
net profit before trading fees	$ 600

The second strategy achieves approximately the same benefit, but without forcing you to sell your stock. After all, if you still believe that the long-term prospects for the stock make it worth holding, the real purpose of the put insurance strategy is to get the profit without giving up the stock. Remember, the put will become more valuable as the stock's market price falls. Using the same example as above, we assume that the stock's price fell to $35 per share. Right before expiration, the put will be worth $500—one point for each point difference between current market value and the put's specified price. That means you can sell the put at $500.

In this case, your profit (before trading fees) is $300, the difference between your sales price of $500 and your original purchase price of $200. Thus, by using a put for insurance, you make a $300 profit and still own the stock. This means that while you originally purchased the stock at $32 per share, the profit from buying the put reduces your basis to $29. The profit is reported as a short-term capital gain for federal tax purposes. Depending on the rules where you live, state income tax might be payable as well.

This illustrates the purpose of a put option used for insurance. It provides partial protection for a momentary profit. This is not a common situation, but it can occur. As a long-term strategist, you should not be looking for opportunities to buy puts, but when extraordinary situations arise, puts can be used to protect your profits.

✦ KEY POINT

Buying puts is acceptable if done for the purpose of ensuring a profit position. This is not the same as speculating as an option buyer.

Creating Higher Profits on Sale

A second strategy for the use of options involves the use of covered calls. These are calls sold by an investor who owns 100 shares of the underlying stock. The concept of selling something as a first step is alien to many investors, more accustomed to the sequence of "buy, hold, sell." With covered calls, the sequence is reversed: "sell, hold, buy."

When you sell a call, you receive the premium value. Thus, you sell the right to the buyer to purchase 100 shares of stock from you, at a specified price, on or before a specified date in the future. Previously, we stated that the risk of buying options was that time worked against the buyer. The opposite is also true. Time works for the seller.

If you were to sell a naked call (also called an uncovered *call*) you would expose yourself to unlimited risk. For example, if you were to sell a call with a strike price of 40 at a time that the stock was selling for $38 per share, the call will not be exercised—as long as the stock's market value remains at or below $40 per share. However, if the stock were suddenly to rise to $50 per share, the call would be exercised. You would be required to deliver 100 shares of stock for $40 per share. Without currently owning the shares, you would have to buy them at current market value ($50 per share) and immediately sell them for $40 per share.

➤ *KEY POINT*

Selling naked calls is extremely risky due to the unlimited risk involved. If the stock rises in value, the naked call writer stands to lose a lot of money.

The sale of a covered call has none of these risks, because you own 100 shares and can deliver them up if the call is exercised. This provides you with an opportunity to control a level of profits or, perhaps, to take intermediate profits without exposing yourself to risk.

Example: You bought 100 shares of stock several years ago at $22 per share. Today, the stock is worth $65. You are willing to sell at that price, but you decide to use the 100 shares for writing a covered call. You sell a call with a strike price of $65 per share, which will expire in three months. You are paid a premium of $500.

When you sell a call against shares you own, you will continue receiving dividends as long as you still own the stock. Four possible outcomes will occur:

1. The stock rises above $65 per share and the option is exercised. In this case, you keep the premium of $500 and give up the stock at $65 per share—even though its current market value is higher. However, this is worthwhile to you because you profit in two ways: the appreciated stock as well as the option premium.
2. The stock rises above $65 per share and you close the call by buying it. You can close out the open option position at any time by buying it. The buy cancels out the original sell position. However, you should recognize that when the stock is valued above the option strike price, the buyer can exercise it at any time. It would make sense to buy if the appreciation in the stock exceeded the appreciated value in the option. For example, let's say that as the expiration date approached, the stock was at $68—three points above strike price—but the option had only appreciated by one point, so that its current value was $600. In this situation, you might be willing to buy the option to close it, taking a $100 loss in the option in exchange for a $300 increase in the value of the stock.

    Such distortions do occur because option premium includes time value, which will gradually disappear as the expiration date approaches. So it is predictable that over a period of time, some of the option's premium will fall, even if the stock is rising. By the date of expiration, only intrinsic value will remain. That means that the stock's current market value will be greater than the strike price of the covered call. If the stock is at $68 per share and the strike price is $65 per share, the call will contain three dollars of intrinsic value.

3. The stock remains at or below the strike price of $65 per share. You close out the call by buying it for less than your original sale price. As long as the stock's market price is lower than the strike price, the option will not be exercised. However, that situation can change quickly, so as long as you have an outstanding call and you are the seller, you are at risk. It often occurs that the current value of the option is lower than the original sale price, so that it can be bought and closed out at a profit. For example, if you sell a call for $500 and it is currently valued at $200, you can purchase it and close out at a $300 profit (before trading fees).

4. The stock remains at or below the strike price of $65 per share. You wait until it expires worthless without taking any action. The maximum profit will be realized if you simply allow the call to expire worthless. This will occur only if the current market value of the stock is at or below strike price as of the expiration date. If your call expires worthless, the entire amount you received on opening the position is yours to keep as profit. In fact, if you want, you can use the same 100 shares to cover another call as soon as the first one expires.

Fundamentalists are long-term thinkers, so option writing should not be the primary strategy for your portfolio. However, when you are willing to let go of stock because it is greatly appreciated, covered call writing is a conservative and profitable strategy. If you consider the possible outcomes, they all end up profitably. First, the call might

🔑 KEY POINT

Covered call writing is a conservative strategy. It eliminates the risk associated with naked call writing. Time works *for* the covered call writer.

expire worthless, so that the premium you receive is all profit. Second, you may close out the position and make a profit on the difference in sale and buy premium levels. Third, your option might be exercised, and you keep the entire premium and earn a capital gain on your appreciated stock.

Anyone getting involved with options should first understand the risk factors involved, study the terminology carefully, and be certain that they understand strategies before making investment decisions. Options are a specialized market and not suitable for many people. However, certain option strategies can be used as one technique for portfolio management, even for the most conservative investor. As a possible starting point, contact the following organizations and request the disclosure documents listed:

Options Clearing Corporation
400 S. LaSalle Street, 24th Floor
Chicago, IL 60605
"OCC Prospectus"
Web site: www.optionsclearing.com

Chicago Board of Exchange
400 S. LaSalle Street
Chicago, IL 60605
"Characteristics and Risks of Standardized Options"
Web site: www.cboe.com (This Web site contains the full text of both the OCC and CBOE disclosure documents.)

Additional Web sites worth checking include the following commercial sites, which provide many descriptions of option strategies, cross-references to other useful sites, and definitions of many different strategies:

www.ies-invest.com
www.covered-calls.com
www.allinthemoney.com
www.e-analytics.com/optdir3.htm (This site contains papers explaining many option strategies.)

Mutual Fund Features

Fundamental analysis has to be applied to all forms of investment. This is true if you buy stocks directly and when you decide to invest through a mutual fund. However, the tests are concerned with the stated objectives of the fund and the track record of the fund's management, rather than with the specific fundamentals of the investments included in the fund's portfolio.

One of the important tests of a mutual fund relates to fees you will be expected to pay for investing. The array of possible fees is very confusing and you will need to understand exactly what fees will be charged in order to efficiently select a fund.

First, you must understand the important distinction between a load fund and a no-load fund. If you select a load fund, you will be required to pay a sales commission. This is deducted from the amount you invest. In comparison, a no-load fund charges no sales fee. So if you invest $100 and the sales charge is 8½ percent, you will have only $91.50 invested in a load fund, whereas all $100 will be working for you in a no-load fund.

Second, all funds charge a management fee to investors. This is a fee used to cover the fund's management's compensation and expenses.

Third is the 12b-1 fee, which some funds charge to pay for its promotional and advertising expenses. In order to qualify as a no-load fund, the mutual fund company may not charge more than 0.25 percent of net asset value as a 12b-1 fee.

Fourth is the back-end load charge, which often is applied only if funds are withdrawn within the first five years or so. This fee, also called the Contingent Deferred Sales Charge (CDSC), is set up to apply on a declining scale. For example, if you withdraw funds during the first year, the load is 5 percent. It declines by one percent per year so that, after the fifth year, it would no longer be assessed.

The fundamentals of mutual fund investing depend largely on management's performance and on the level of fees charged. Comparisons are difficult because different funds assess varying kinds of fees that cannot be easily equated, so a concerted effort to make true comparisons will be required.

A lot of emphasis is placed on what would have happened if you had invested a set sum of money at some point in the past and reinvested dividends. A more revealing analysis is a study of how fund performance compared to varying market conditions, especially when the market as a whole was on a downward trend. Mutual funds are the most popular form of investing among Americans. As of 1998, 40 million people—one of every three households—owned shares in one or more mutual funds. Total assets for those funds exceeded $3 trillion.

Identifying risks in mutual funds is difficult because of the emphasis on actual past performance—in other words, market value of fund shares. In other words, the means for selection is based on largely technical signs, how funds have performed against measurements like the Dow Jones Industrial Average or the Standard & Poor's 500. Did the fund beat those indexes? This is the key means for selection. You should want to select mutual funds based on fees charged as well as management's historical performance record. When you invest in a mutual fund, you are trusting management to use fundamental analysis in order to pick good stocks—assuming that the type of fund also matches your investment goals. If you are interested in long-term growth, you should determine in advance that the fund is designed for the same purpose. Many funds emphasize current income from dividends and interest, and invest in high-yield stocks and bonds, or take a very conservative point of view, or buy in specific industries or sectors.

Unfortunately, even if you select a fund using a set of criteria, there are no guarantees that future performance will match past performance. The best approach may be to select funds that have performed above average consistently in the past, even when the market was doing poorly by other measurements. Information concerning the fund's investment objectives and policies, experience of management, fees and charges, and past performance, will all be found in the fund prospectus, which should always be obtained and read before investing. While reading the prospectus is advice given in all cases by professionals because it is required by law, it is important to read a mutual fund prospectus (and the prospectus for other types of investments) before investing.

CHAPTER 14

Valuable Techniques
for the Savvy Investor

*E*very investor deals with the same market. That is to say, no one really starts out with an unfair advantage or disadvantage in the stock market. The uncertainty, opportunity, and risk applies to everyone.

Those who learn how to maximize opportunities and minimize risks ultimately will outperform the market. Why? Because the majority of investors, including large institutions with full-time professional analysts, fail to use the right fundamental tools, and fail to act on the right information, even when it is obvious. This raises a few interesting questions. If the wrong way to respond is so obvious, why do people continue to act as they do? Why don't people recognize the universal truths of the market and act accordingly?

The problem is that there are many schools of thought about what strategies are right or wrong in the market. People continue to act as they do because the errors made in investing are not as obvious as we might think. And there are no universal truths in the market. Not everyone agrees with the ideas and suggestions offered in this book. For example, there is great comfort and reassurance in the up and down movements of the Dow Jones Industrial Average (DJIA). Many investors and analysts choose to believe that the DJIA is the market, and that watching its fluctuations provides reliable indications of how to time personal investment decisions.

It is everyone's right to believe as they wish, and to disagree with others. Fundamentalists struggle to overcome the desire for easy

209

solutions and answers, recognizing that identification of truth often is the result of hard work, and the process of finding knowledge is very dull, compared to the more exciting technical approach to investing. A contrarian constantly questions the majority thinking in the market, and would prefer to doubt commonly held beliefs than to simply go along. You will discover that there is a certain sense of danger in questioning commonly held beliefs, even when your sense of logic requires that you disagree with what most people think to be right. Oscar Wilde observed, "To believe is very dull. To doubt is intensely engrossing."

The contrarian needs to overcome more than the majority point of view. Remember, it is not just that most people are wrong; most people don't even get to the point of questioning their own beliefs. To succeed as a contrarian, you also need to develop a strong and unyielding belief in what you know to be right and logical. Scientific, realistic research is rare in the market. The majority believes in many things that are misleading, false, inaccurate, and unreliable. As unpopular as it might be to so state, reliance on the DJIA is one of those things. The movements in today's averages tell you absolutely nothing about the market; about the individual stocks in the averages, or about how or when you should make investment decisions.

✦ KEY POINT

If you merely begin to question the basic beliefs held in the market, you will be far ahead of most people, who never get to that point at all.

The specific techniques you use in managing your stock market investments should depend on specific circumstances, your ability to tolerate risk, and the current market conditions. The basic beliefs you apply—fundamental versus technical, or contrarian versus consensus thinking—serve as the foundation for your strategic approach. The techniques you select and use are the action steps by which you put your beliefs to work in portfolio management.

Reinvesting Profits

The first technique worth considering is the reinvestment of profits, a form of compounding your return. A study of the effects of compound interest makes the point. When you leave earnings to accumulate, the effect is dramatic. The same is true in investing.

Mutual fund investors can easily apply the principle of compounded return simply by instructing management to reinvest all dividends, interest, and capital gains in additional shares. This is one of the reasons mutual funds are widely popular investment vehicles; the ability to leave funds at work in compounded, reinvested form, adds up to ever-increasing profits over time. Direct ownership of stock does not provide for the same universal level of convenience. Many corporations allow stockholders to reinvest dividends in partial share purchases often without additional brokerage fees. Look for stocks offering DRIPs (dividend reinvestment plans), direct ownership makes reinvestment difficult.

The importance of reinvesting your capital and keeping it at work should not be ignored. Just as the interest you pay on mortgages and other loans has a compounding effect, so does investment earnings. In the long term, it is the accumulated benefit of keeping capital at work that adds up to significant profits, rather than the regular deposit of additional funds. The combined effect of putting money aside and reinvesting earnings is the real answer to wealth building over a lifetime.

🏃 *KEY POINT*

Investment performance—yield and capital gains—is only a part of the profit picture. It is the compounded effect of reinvestment over many years that adds up to truly impressive overall profit.

Dollar Cost Averaging

One good method for establishing and managing an ongoing program of regular investing is dollar cost averaging. This means that the same amount of capital is invested in a portfolio at regular intervals, regardless of the share price. Dollar cost averaging tends to average out the overall share price paid for securities. When the stock's market price is rising, the average share price is invariably lower than the current market price. And when the stock's market price is falling, the average share cost under dollar cost averaging is continually reduced, through dollar cost averaging, to reduce the overall paper loss.

Dollar cost averaging is popular because it reduces the risk of loss while giving investors a formula for recurring investment. It works well in situations where the actual dollar amount does not matter, such as in mutual funds. In fact, most funds specify a minimum investment amount, and that amount buys whatever number of fractional shares are available at the current price. The combination of dollar cost averaging and dividend reinvestment is appropriate as well as popular in the mutual fund industry.

✍ KEY POINT

Dollar cost averaging is a technique for regular, disciplined investing. It enables you to overcome short-term tendencies to vary an otherwise sensible investment strategy.

The direct purchaser of stock faces a problem with dollar cost averaging. Unless you are willing to pay higher trading fees for odd lot purchases, dollar cost averaging is not a very practical way to invest. Because of the trading mechanisms and practices of the market, direct purchasers of stock are more likely to purchase round lots of stock rather than trying to regiment their buying practices. While dollar cost averaging has a certain mathematical appeal to the mutual fund investor, it creates problems in the direct purchase of stocks.

Setting Goals to Ensure Profits and Limit Losses

Most investors start out understanding their investment goals, but soon forget to make decisions guided by those goals. Virtually all professional advisers—stockbrokers and financial planners, for example—recommend that their clients set and follow goals. However, there is no means for follow-up to ensure that such advice is taken. It is up to you to remember to put fundamental information first, to put technical information in perspective, and to analyze sources and data to determine its validity. Finally, it is up to you to practice goal setting as a first step, and then to ensure that you guide yourself by your goals.

Be aware of the obvious rules most people break. These include the following:

Failing to define. To succeed as an investor, you need to define the different sources of information and whether or not you assign validity. You also need to know why you are investing and what you hope to achieve. For example, some investors hope to save up for a down payment on a home, young families want to save for their children's college education, and middle-aged investors are starting to think about retirement. All of these dissimilar goals affect the types of investments you select.

Also define risks. Remember that risks define not only the chances you take, but the potential for returns. Conservative, low-yielding investments are going to contain less market risk; aggressive growth stocks have greater appreciation potential but also contain greater risk. Your risk tolerance should define the types of investments appropriate in your case.

Ignoring or forgetting risk. It is easy when investing in the stock market to become preoccupied with the various forms of analysis, the fast-moving and changing tone of trading, and the abundance of information in varying quality; and to forget that all decisions should be equated to risk, and specifically to your personal risk tolerance. This is an attribute you need to define and then use as a guideline in all decision making.

🔑 KEY POINT

Risk is everything. Fundamentals point to specific risks and to changes in financial status that translate to changes in risk. All of your investment decisions should hinge on how much risk is involved—even including the risk of doing nothing.

Reacting to short-term information. No matter how careful you are to define yourself as a fundamentalist, the rumors and short-term opportunities are out there in abundance. It is very easy to get sidetracked by the promise of immediate opportunity, by the idea that you can beat the averages, or by the idea that a prediction might be right this time. Always keep your vision on your long-term goal and try to ignore the momentary tendencies of the market.

Giving in to panic or greed. The two most common emotions during times of dramatic changes in the market are panic and greed. As markets fall unexpectedly, the herd mentality calls for a panic reaction. Investors dump stocks as they fall, hoping to cut losses, not stopping to realize that a rebound is virtually inevitable. The same is true when markets begin to climb suddenly. The greed reaction is to overbuy, forget about risk tolerance levels and long-term goals, ignore the importance of diversification, and want to get in on the big profit. At some point, the greed reaction ends up in a correction and people lose money.

Resist both panic and greed and you will be less likely to experience the most common causes of loss in the stock market: making decisions for the wrong reasons and without stopping to think of the long term.

✦ KEY POINT

Panic and greed are the two factors most likely to lead to losses. If you ignore these forces, you are going to be light years ahead of most people.

Picking the wrong stock for the wrong reasons. The classic mistake made by investors involves selecting the wrong stock—one that defies the risk tolerance criteria, the goals, and the fundamentals an investor has been studying. All of that work is meaningless if the actual decision is made without depending on the data to back it up. Yet thousands of investors can look back and identify a time when they have done that very thing: buying stock they should not buy, and losing money because of it.

Changing goals when circumstances change. Setting goals is important because goals define everything else: the best investment strategy, the right investments, and your risk tolerance. However, be aware that goals change. One plan is not forever. The major occurrences in life require a reevaluation of goals. These include going to college, starting a business, marriage, having children, divorce, retiring, and death, among others. Each change in circumstances is accompanied by a change in investment requirements, the need for insurance, the importance of safety, the time you have to reach your goals, and all other aspects of investing. When concentrating on the fundamentals of your portfolio, don't forget to review the equally important fundamentals of your own life.

✦ *KEY POINT*

Change is the nature of the market. Therefore, strategies need to be reviewed and replaced as conditions change.

Becoming impatient. Last but not least is the widespread problem of impatience. Succeeding in the stock market requires time. If you expect to make a profit overnight but that doesn't happen, it does not mean the approach is wrong, nor that your strategies are untimely. It means only that you need to give it time. Fundamentals promising future profits may be correct, but those indicators also need time to season. The very nature of growth itself requires patience, because growth is a gradual process. Accountants recognize the problems in forecasting growth when it occurs too quickly, in advance of capital structure's ability to finance it, or inconsistently from one year to the next. Permanent growth is gradual and steady. Just as a child's height grows gradually over many years, expanded profitability of a corporation is reflected in long-term fundamental signs and patient management and timing of expansion.

Avoiding the Pitfalls

As a follower of fundamental analysis, you already know that the market is not a roulette wheel, even though that kind of approach is popular and common. You know that depending on the financial

⚓ KEY POINT

If the market worked the way many people think, they may as well take their chances at a casino. Informed decisions overcome the speculative choices that people often end up making.

information about a company is the real key to success. A long history of belief in the fundamentals has established this basic truth. It is supported by many analysts, even those who do not follow the fundamental guidelines. Investors who succeed over the long term are invariably dedicated to fundamental information and have learned to use it.

Even so, you need to maintain a perspective on fundamental analysis. It is to be used for the development of opinions, strategies, and beliefs. It is not a sure-fire method for always beating the market. All investors have losses mixed in with their gains, a fact supporting the principle of diversification. You need to monitor your portfolio continually after making a decision to buy. A hold decision should not be considered as permanent, because situations—both for the company whose stock you own and for yourself—change with time.

How do you keep fundamental analysis in perspective? Try the following ideas.

Constantly question with a fresh point of view. Even if you are convinced that the techniques you select provide you with solid information, and that your current portfolio contains excellent stock selections, remember to perform periodic reviews in a critical manner. Look at today's information with a buyer's eye. Would you buy the same stock today? If not, why not? What has changed, and should that change lead you to a sell decision?

Continue reviewing financial reports. Like everything else, financial status of a publicly held company may change over time. In fact, change is certain. Some industries that are popular and strong today will probably be weak and unprofitable in a few years. You need to look for changes using fundamentals, and to recognize when trends begin to turn.

Maintain your program of trend analysis. Never depend on a single trend, but use combinations of trends to confirm apparent changes in financial strength or profitability. Keep the analysis going, and remember that the actual selection of a portfolio is not the end of the process. It is only a step. A program designed to provide you with reliable information is to be used for buying, but also to evaluate a hold position, and to indicate if and when you should sell a stock.

Review the trend mix you use and be willing to change it.
Some trends that work today will not work in a few years, for a variety of reasons. For example, a company might change its own mix of lines of business through a series of acquisitions. Thus, informative trends in one period might not reveal much in the next; or a trend's direction might be distorted and you won't know how to evaluate the information. When a company makes a big change, that could make it necessary for you to start over with your trend watching.

Pay attention to the gossip, news, and rumors of the market.
Although the day-to-day rumor mill of the market should not be used to make decisions, they should not be ignored. The mood of the market has much to do with pricing of stocks, at least in the short term, and the fundamentals have everything to do with growth potential in the long term. So while your emphasis should be in the selection of good, long-term growth stocks, the immediate direction and mood of the market is interesting as well.

Don't discount technical information altogether.   Remember that some technical indicators can be used in conjunction with fundamentals. Some, like price-earnings ratio, are really not pure technical indicators, but technimental in nature, because they combine price (technical) with earnings (fundamental). Such information is valuable. Tests of volatility can be useful as well as a means for researching further into the reasons for the volatility; and as a method for judging the market risk of a stock. A study of a stock's chart provides you with support and resistance information and long-term study of price patterns can enable you to predict a stock's market personality over the long term—useful information even for the dedicated fundamentalist.

Market investors—even those who believe in fundamentals—often act on their own intuitive sense of what is going on in the market. The hunch is widely used for impulsive decisions to buy or sell, or to change strategies. As dangerous as it is to bet on a hunch, you should not ignore a strong one when it occurs. Remember that the market is

> ## ✎ *KEY POINT*
>
> Get information wherever it can be found. You will have insight
> into the mood of the market by watching the technical as well as
> the fundamental. Don't ignore information because it is not fun-
> damental because that will prevent you from learning.

overloaded with information and you have to process such a large
amount of raw data that you don't really know how much of it is useful. One of the great difficulties in the market is deciding how to focus,
to narrow the range of information you consider valid.

In that environment, your hunch might be an informed recognition
of combined facts that mean something important. Our brains have
analytical abilities that are not well understood, and a study has shown
that what we often attribute to hunches is really considered opinion
based on information. Intuition may work as a form of confirmation.
Just as you should use one trend to confirm what you think you see in
another, your intuition could work as a form of confirmation for what
you already know, based on a study of financial information. For example, you might sense after many years that a particular company's ability to grow has peaked out, and future earnings will not expand. This
sense could be intuitive if not indicated directly by trends, but it also
confirms your observations over many years of studying that company's financial statements. You know some things intuitively, as Laurie
Nadel observed in *Sixth Sense* (Prentice Hall Press, 1990):

> Intuitive knowing is qualitatively different from other mental
> processes. It reflects your sensitivity to internal messages as well as
> to your external environment and can be described as an openness to
> flashes of insight that come as wholes.

The challenge is to think clearly when evaluating information and
determining whether to consider it as valid. The comfort you can take
in the fundamentals is that they are specific and exact. You may interpret the numbers as you wish, but the use of fundamentals, expressed
as ratios and studied as entries in continuing trends, demonstrates what
is happening in the company. Intuition is yet another sort of information: it is not independent from the knowledge you acquire through the
fundamentals; it can be used as a confirming source of opinion; and you
may decide to act on that opinion.

⚓ KEY POINT

Clear thinking is compatible with intuition, which can be a useful method for confirming what you already suspect.

It is a mistake to ignore hunches entirely, to be a pure scientist and to refuse to acknowledge what is occurring beyond the pure science of fundamentals. This is why you should keep one eye on the rumors and gossip of the market. Keeping in touch with the perspective and sentiment of the market may lead you to decisions you would not have been able to develop from a pure study of fundamental indicators.

Becoming a Successful Investor

Whatever strategy you employ to manage your portfolio—to select stocks, hold them, trade, and make your goals into realities—the ultimate test will be profits. If you meet your goals, then you will succeed as an investor. If you do not, then your strategy and actions will prove to have been wrong.

The key question concerning the decision about which approach to take should be: Have you ever met someone who adhered to fundamental principles and lost over the long term? The point is, when you hear about people who lost in the market, it is worth examining what they did and how they lost. While fundamentalists can lose just like anyone else taking a risk, most of the unexpected short-term losses you hear about result from speculative activity. This includes investing without research and only on a rumor, taking someone else's advice without discovering the source, abandoning a sensible policy to follow the herd, selling in a panic, investing on indicators that have no real meaning, employing strategies without really understanding

⚓ KEY POINT

The majority of losses in the market result from easily identified mistakes and those can be avoided.

them, or ignoring fundamentals that (at least in hindsight) are glaringly obvious.

All of these mistakes are likely to expose you to short-term market risk. The truly studious, serious investor does not make those mistakes. If you are intent on succeeding in the stock market, and if you would prefer to select your own stocks rather than trusting a mutual fund's management, then you will need to use the fundamentals. Furthermore, if you follow a sensible course and set rules for yourself—not only about buying, but also about when and why to hold or to sell a stock— then you have a much better than average chance of profiting from your investments.

Setting policies enables you to maximize profits and minimize losses. You may be certain about one thing. Both profits and losses are going to occur in the market, and you will probably experience both. There are steps you can take, however, to ensure that your hard work, research, and sincere belief in the fundamentals will ultimately pay off.

Three suggested simple but logical investment and risk management policies that probably will enhance your overall profits are:

1. *Identify the reasons you will sell.* Fundamentalists are supposed to identify the best possible growth prospects, and then diversify their portfolios and invest in those stocks for the long term. This is a simple strategy. However, remember that things change. Watch the trends you choose, and be willing to sell a stock if today's financial strength turns into financial weakness. Some industry leaders will be replaced in the future; some growing companies will plateau and cease growing; many companies that are strong today will be obsolete in the future as new competitors and new technology change the way that people buy. Be aware that even the fundamentals have to be monitored so that important financial changes can be recognized as early as possible.

2. *Set analytical criteria and review regularly.* The trends you choose to watch are all-important, but of equal importance is the method you select in your review. If your analysis is not producing reliable information, then it is time to replace one set of trends with another, more informative one. Because a company's financial status changes over time, some trends cease to reveal what is really going on. You need to be aware of this, and to recognize when the information in a trend is not really revealing anything of interest. Constantly look at all of the ratios to

spot which ones have more interesting trends and may be properly included in your analytical program.

3. *Keep an open mind to the possibility of change. It is certain to occur.* Finally, be aware that even the strongest, most solidly managed company of today might be entirely obsolete tomorrow. History can teach us a lot. The time when railroads and steel companies dominated the market has long passed. Likewise, the makeup of the DJIA has changed since its inception. The changes reflect a changing society and economy; new technology; and a move away from manufacturing to service. In the future, it is virtually certain that today's technology and consumer interests will be replaced with something new that has not yet been invented.

Trends are visible everywhere. Consider the impact of the Internet. Serious investors should have access to the Internet, if only for the convenience of quotation checking. Many investors trade on the Internet, or at the very least use it for research into companies. In the future, it is likely that modern television, telephone, and communications technology will be replaced by something more instant, more affordable, and more efficient—and that these new technologies will be available through the Internet.

If you apply this type of social development to your understanding of the market, you will better comprehend the nature of investing successfully. There is no one set formula or strategy that will work forever. Change defines and characterizes the market. You need to be able to change, to consider new and even radical ideas and strategies to keep ahead of the majority, and to better develop fundamental approaches to portfolio management.

In the long run, the successful investor is one who is willing to put in the time for research and comparison; who takes the time to become proficient at interpreting financial information; and who is willing to compile trends and watch them from month to month. This requires commitment and work. It translates to profits in the future, which occur over time and not all at once. The allure of getting rich suddenly and without any work will always appeal to some people, and a few make it. Most, however, end up losing money as a reflection of inexperience and wishful thinking.

You will succeed in the market as long as you use fundamental analysis—not only as your primary means for picking stocks, but also for the subsequent decisions about when or if to sell. The allure of immediate profit, of finding an easy way, and of winning the prediction game, are widely popular and fun, but the fundamentals—dependable but requiring greater patience—have the advantage over the years: Fundamentals show you the path to consistent profit and to meet your goals.

accrual basis accounting A system for recording transactions that recognizes income in the period earned, regardless of when it is received, and that recognizes costs and expenses in the period incurred, regardless of when paid.

accumulated depreciation The sum of depreciation claimed during all current and past years; the total is reflected on the balance sheet as a reduction of the cost basis of noncurrent assets.

acid test Alternative name for *quick assets ratio.*

annual dividend per share The dollar amount of dividend paid per year per share of a company's stock; it is reported in the daily stock listings.

annualized return The return on an investment on a per-year basis.

assets The properties and accounts owned by a company, including "current" assets (for example, cash, accounts receivable, inventory, property, plant, and equipment); deferred assets; and intangible assets. The total value of all assets is equal to the sum of liabilities plus shareholders' equity.

auction marketplace The open stock exchange, where stock is bought and sold competitively. Buyers compete with one another for the lowest prices and sellers compete to obtain the highest possible prices.

back-end load A charge against mutual fund assets assessed at the time shares are sold, but often charged only if withdrawals occur within a specified number of years from initial investment.

balance sheet A financial statement reporting the current value of assets, liabilities, and shareholders' equity as of a specified date, usually the end of a quarter or year. The date of the balance sheet corresponds with the ending date of the period being reported in the statement of income that accompanies the balance sheet. The sum of all assets reported on the balance sheet is equal to the total of liabilities plus shareholders' equity.

banking earnings The accounting practice of deferring a portion of earnings in an exceptionally good year, so that profits will be smoothly reported over future periods.

basic earnings per share Calculation of net earnings, divided by the number of outstanding shares of common stock, before considering the effects of dilution.

bear market A general market condition characterized by pessimism, falling prices in stocks, and a belief that the near-term future will see lower market prices for stocks.

beta A measurement of volatility, comparing historical price movement of the stock to the market as a whole.

bond A debt security issued by a corporation with a contractual promise to pay a set rate of interest and to repay the principal at a predetermined date.

223

bond ratio A ratio showing the portion of total capitalization represented by bonds. To compute the ratio, divide the dollar value of bonds by total capitalization; the result is expressed as a percentage.

book value per share The intrinsic value of a company's stock, calculated by dividing tangible capital dollar value by the number of outstanding shares of common stock.

bottom line The net profit of a company.

breadth index A measurement of advances and declines in a trading period.

breakout In technical analysis, the movement of a stock's market value above resistance level or below support level.

bull market General market condition characterized by optimism, rising prices in stocks, and a belief that the near-term future will see higher market prices for stocks.

business cycles The patterns of fluctuation in growth patterns experienced by business caused by overall economic and financial trends, competitive forces, and the nature of supply and demand. Cycles are predictable in patterns but not always in durations.

call An option giving the owner of a call the right to buy 100 shares of stock at a specified price by a specified deadline.

capital stock The value of an outstanding share of stock at the time it was issued.

capitalization The combined sources of capital, consisting of debt capital (liabilities) and equity capital (capital stock and retained earnings).

cash flow Increases and decreases in working capital affected by fluctuating income and/or expenses.

cash flow statement Alternative name for the *statement of cash flow*.

common stock ratio A ratio showing the portion of total capitalization represented by common stock and retained earnings. To compute, add the dollar value of common stock plus retained earnings and divide by total capitalization; the result is expressed as a percentage.

contingent liabilities Potential liabilities known about at the time a financial statement is prepared, which might or might not become actual liabilities in the future.

contrarian An investor who believes that the majority of investors is usually wrong, and that decisions should never be made because the majority follows that course of thinking.

convertible bond A form of bond (debt investment) that can be converted to common stock (equity investment) if the investor so chooses, either at a specified price per share or by a specified deadline.

convertible preferred stock Stock that can be converted to common stock if the investor wishes, at a set price per share or by a specified deadline.

convertible securities Bond or preferred stock that can be converted to common stock if the investor so chooses.

cook the books Term describing accounting practices that misrepresent the true financial status of a company to achieve a desired result, such as showing higher profits or more consistent reports from one period to another. The practice involves the posting of transactions before or after their true periods, creative accounting procedures, and other practices not acceptable under standards of accounting and auditing practice.

cost of sales The costs associated with generating reported sales, including merchandise, direct labor, and other costs attributed to current sales activity.

covered calls A call option that is sold when the seller also owns 100 shares of the underlying stock.

current assets A company's cash assets and assets that are convertible to cash within one year. This classification includes cash accounts, accounts receivable (net of reserve for bad debts), inventory, and marketable securities.

current interest rate The rate being earned on a bond based on its current market value; that value varies with the degree of premium or discount value of the bond.

current portion of long-term debt Those liabilities that are payable within the next 12 months, including accounts and taxes payable, and the current portion (12 months' payments) of notes payable and current liabilities.

current ratio A ratio that tests the strength of a company's working capital. Current assets are divided by current liabilities and the result is expressed as a factor, *x* to *y*.

debenture A corporate bond without any collateral; its value is based on the reputation and financial strength of the issuer.

debt/equity ratio A ratio showing the percentage of total shareholders' equity represented by long-term debt. This important fundamental test shows the degree of capitalization that is derived from debt rather than from equity.

debt investments Investments that involve making capital available to others in exchange for interest, through savings accounts, loans, or bonds.

deferred assets Payments that will be assigned as expenses in a later period, but that are paid in advance and temporarily set up as assets on the balance sheet.

deferred credits Deferred income listed in the liability section of the balance sheet.

depreciation An annual deduction for a portion of the value of property, plant, and equipment.

diluted earnings per share A calculation of earnings per share. Add conversion value of preferred stock and convertible bonds to net profits, then divide the result by the number of outstanding shares of common stock that would exist after full conversion; the result is expressed as a dollar value per share.

dilution The reduction in book value per share of stock that occurs when new shares are sold.

direct costs Costs related directly to sales.

discount A value lower than par value; the decreased market value of a bond resulting from its interest rate and safety rating.

discount rate The loan interest rate charged by the Federal Reserve Bank to its member banks.

diversification An investor's practice of spreading risk by placing capital in different stocks, different industries, or dissimilar investments, so that a loss caused by one factor will not adversely affect the entire portfolio.

dividend payout ratio A ratio showing the percentage of net profits paid out in dividends on common stock, after reducing net profits by the amount of dividends paid on preferred stock.

dividend yield A stock's daily percentage summary of yield, calculated by dividing annual dividend per share by the day's closing stock price.

dollar cost averaging A system of investing in which an unchanging dollar amount is invested at regular intervals, regardless of share price.

Dow Theory A theory contending that a primary market trend—one that will last for a year or more—will follow the movements in at least two of the three Dow Jones

Averages (industrials, transportation, and utilities). The theory is based on the belief that trends follow movements set by the indexes.

earnings per share The latest reported net earnings, divided by the number of outstanding shares of common stock; one of the most widely used forms for reporting earnings, also called *basic earnings per share* and distinguished from diluted earnings per share.

economic indicators Statistical indexes, rates, and other measurements of national financial and social trends, used to predict overall business climate and growth patterns.

efficient market A theory about the stock market stating that the current prices of stocks reflect all that is known about the company at that moment, and that new information is reflected immediately in changes to that stock's market price.

equity investments Investments that involve ownership of shares or units, through purchase of stock or mutual fund shares.

expiration date The date on which an option expires, after which the option cannot be exercised.

extraordinary items Unusual transactions showing up on a company's financial statement that will not recur every year. Extraordinary items may be restructuring, the writing off of losses due to changes in valuation methods, settlement of lawsuits, exceptionally high profit or loss from foreign exchange, or similar transactions not common for the company.

face value Alternative name for *par value*.

federal funds rate The rate charged by the Federal Reserve to member banks when excess reserve loans are made from one bank to another.

fixed assets Alternative name for *noncurrent assets*.

full disclosure The principle of providing to investors all information required to make informed buying decisions, normally applied to new listings and specifically to information included in the prospectus.

fundamental analysis A method of research that studies basic financial information to forecast profits, supply and demand, industry strength, management ability, and other intrinsic matters affecting a stock's market value and growth potential.

gross margin The percentage of gross profit (sales minus direct costs) to sales, which should remain fairly consistent when sales rise or fall.

gross profit The profit remaining after direct costs are subtracted from sales, but before any expenses are deducted.

growth in earnings per share A ratio comparing current earnings per share to the same ratio in a base year; it is used to track rates of growth for the company.

growth in sales A ratio comparing current sales levels to sales in a base year; it identifies the percentage of increase in volume.

inflation An increase in prices, also reflected as a decrease in purchasing power, the rate of which is measured by the Consumer Price Index (CPI).

initial public offering (IPO) A corporation's first sale of stock to the public.

insider An officer or director of a company, anyone who owns more than 10 percent of a corporation's voting stock and his or her immediate family members, or anyone who has information about a company that is not available to other investors.

institutional investors Investors other than individuals, such as pension plans, banks, mutual funds, and life insurance companies. Because such investors buy large blocks of shares, they often are given substantial trading cost discounts.

intangible assets A company's assets reported on the balance sheet that have no tangible or physical value. Intangible assets are excluded from the calculation of book value per share.

interest coverage A ratio comparing operating profit to interest obligation on bonds; used to determine how well those profits provide for the cost of long-term debt capitalization.

intrinsic value A portion of option premium reflecting only the difference between an option's strike price and the current market price of the stock. Intrinsic value exists when market value is greater than a call's strike price, or when market value is less than a put's strike price.

inventory turnover A ratio summarizing the average number of times that inventory was replaced during a period of time. It reflects whether management is able to control inventory levels and use working capital effectively.

investment grade Bonds rated in one of the top four rating classifications, appropriately safe, and unlikely to miss interest payments or go into default.

junk bonds Bonds classified below investment grade and considered highly speculative.

lagging economic indicators Statistical information reported by the Department of Commerce used to confirm anticipated economic trends showing up in the leading indicators, including seven indicators representing trends in employment, business inventory levels, prime interest rate and credit levels, and changes in the Consumer Price Index.

law of large numbers A concept in probability and logic stating that if you study a large enough sample, the outcomes of any statistical tests are highly predictable.

leading economic indicators Statistical information developed to monitor the trends in the American economy, including primary indicators representing trends in: productivity; employment; orders and sales in business; purchase of property, plant, and equipment; housing permits; business inventory levels; the stock market; the money supply; and estimates of what consumers expect.

liabilities Obligations of the company, including current liabilities (due and payable within 12 months), long-term liabilities, and deferred credits.

load fund A mutual fund that charges a sales commission against amounts invested, which is then paid to the salesperson placing investors' capital in the fund.

long-term liabilities The dollar amount of loans, notes, and other amounts due and payable as debts, but not due within the coming 12 months.

management fee A fee charged annually to a fund's investors to cover management compensation and expenses; such a fee is usually between .5 percent and 1 percent of the fund's net asset value.

market risk The risk associated with a stock's market price; that the price will fall and the stock will lose value.

monetary aggregates The total money supply, including all money market instruments, deposits, and currency in circulation.

money market The market for short-term debt instruments, including treasury bills, certificates of deposit, money market funds and accounts, bankers acceptances, and short-term corporate and government notes, as well as others.

money supply A measurement of the amount of money in circulation, consisting of cash and checking balances held in financial institutions and in circulation.

moving average An averaging technique in which the field being averaged is maintained at the same number; the oldest value in the field is dropped off when the newest value in the field is added on.

naked call (Also called a *uncovered call)* A call sold without a corresponding ownership of 100 shares of the underlying stock, exposing the seller to the risk that the call will be exercised and the seller must pay more for the shares to cover the call than the selling price stated in the call.

net margin The percentage of net profit compared to sales for a corporation, either for the quarter or for an entire year. Compute by dividing net profit by total sales; the result is expressed as a percentage.

net profit (Also called *net profit after taxes)* The profit realized (or "bottom line") after all income is calculated and all costs, expenses, and income taxes are deducted from total income.

net profit before taxes The profit realized when all income, costs, and expenses are included. Income and expenses other than from sales—such as profit or loss from foreign exchange, and interest income and expense—are factored into the net profit before taxes.

net profit from operations Alternative name for *operating profit.*

no-load fund A mutual fund that does not charge a sales commission against investments. Such a fund usually is selected by people buying over-the-counter and not investing through a commissioned salesperson or financial planner.

nominal interest rate The stated, contractual rate of interest paid on bonds.

noncurrent assets Property, plant, and equipment owned by the company, including real estate, autos and trucks, machinery and equipment, office equipment, and other assets subject to depreciation.

odd lot A lot of stock less than 100 shares.

odd lot theory A theory based on the belief that odd lot traders are usually wrong about market direction. When odd lot buy volume increases, it is seen as a contrarian signal to sell; when odd lot sale volume increases, it is taken as a signal to buy.

operating profit (Also called *net profit from operations*) A company's profit from selling its primary goods or services, after accounting for costs and expenses but before allowing for extraordinary items (unrelated income and expenses) or for income taxes due and payable on the profit.

options Intangible investments giving the owner the right to buy or to sell 100 shares of a specified stock at a specified price, by a specified date.

PE ratio (price-earnings ratio) A basic indicator of market value for stock; it compares the market price per share to the latest reported earnings per share.

par value (Also called *face value)* The face value of a bond; the amount that will be paid to the investor on maturity.

parity A condition where common stock is of equal value to a convertible security.

preferred stock A form of stock that normally does not include voting rights (unlike common stock). Holders of preferred stock have priority in the case of liquidation, and will be paid before holders of common stock. If the corporation is unable to make full dividend payments, holders of preferred stock are paid up to a full dividend prior to any monies being apportioned to holders of common stock.

preferred stock ratio A ratio showing the portion of total capitalization represented by preferred stock. To compute, divide the dollar value of preferred stock by total capitalization; the result is expressed as a percentage.

premium A share's value that is greater than par value; the increased market value of a bond resulting from its interest rate payable and safety rating.

pretax profit A company's net profit before taxes.

price-earnings ratio See *PE ratio.*

primary earnings per share The calculated earnings per share involving a straight comparison between net earnings and outstanding shares of common stock, without considering the effects of dilution in the event that conversion rights of convertible securities investors were to be exercised; usually referred to simply as earnings per share.

prime rate The rate charged by lenders to their customers having the highest credit ratings.

profit and loss statement Alternative name for *statement of income.*

property, plant, and equipment Those assets purchased by a corporation that are subject to depreciation over several years; they cannot be written off as expenses in the year purchased.

put An option giving the owner the right to sell 100 shares of stock at a specified price by a specified deadline, regardless of the stock's current market value at the time the put is exercised.

quick assets ratio (Also called *acid test*) A ratio comparing current assets (excluding inventory) to current liabilities.

random walk A theory about the stock market stating that stock price changes are not related to market forces but are based on the random application of new information.

ratio An expression of the relationship between two or more values, for example, the PE (price-earnings) ratio.

recovery periods The groupings of time mandated by the tax code over which depreciation can be claimed for specific classifications of property, plant, and equipment.

resistance level The price that technicians believe represents the highest price a stock is likely to reach under current conditions.

retail investors Individuals trading in the stock market, so-called because they do not trade in large enough blocks to be granted the substantial block trading discounts given to institutional investors.

retained earnings Part of the company's shareholders' equity representing net profits for all years accumulated through the current year, minus federal income taxes and dividends paid out.

return on equity A ratio comparing a company's net income to its shareholders' averaged equity, to arrive at the return on total equity invested during a given year.

risk tolerance The level of risk that an investor is willing to assume.

round lots Trading increments of 100 (or multiples of 100) shares; the normal trading mode used in the stock market.

sentiment indicator A type of indicator used to measure investor attitude, belief, mood, or opinion, as opposed to one that measures a financial or point value or reveals changes in an index.

shareholders' equity The value of the company; the difference between assets and liabilities, and the company's total dollar worth including capital stock and retained earnings.

simple average A method for computing average where the field of values is added together, then divided by the total number of values.

statement of cash flow A financial statement summarizing the company's uses of cash income and current assets, and its uses of its cash expenses and current liabilities; a summary of the changes in working capital expressed for the fiscal year.

statement of income The financial statement summarizing activity during a period of time, usually a full year or the latest quarter. Included are sales, costs of goods sold, general expenses, and net profit.

strike price The set price at which an option can be exercised, regardless of the underlying stock's market price at the time the option is exercised.

sugar bowl The practice of establishing an overly large loss reserve in a good year, with the intention of reducing that reserve in future years so that profits can be reported more consistently than they actually occur.

support level The price that technicians believe represents the lowest price a stock is likely to reach under current conditions.

technical analysis The study of nonintrinsic trends, notably stock price chart patterns, popularity of stocks and industry groups, and the psychological forces in the market, as opposed to the dollars and cents of financial information.

technimental analysis Any form of information based on technical indicators but containing fundamental information as its base, or combining elements of technical and fundamental analysis.

time value A portion of an option's premium that reflects the value between today and expiration; time value will evaporate as expiration date approaches.

total capitalization The combination of bonds and other long-term obligations such as preferred stock, and the combination of common stock and retained earnings.

total return The return on an investment taking into account not only growth in value, but dividends or interest earned as well.

trading symbol A company's abbreviated alphabetical symbol, used for stock listings, to report transactions, and for placing orders.

treasury stock Stock that is purchased by the issuing corporation and retired. Treasury stock has no voting rights. No dividends are paid unless it is subsequently reissued.

trend The direction or orientation of financial results; the line on a graph showing how financial relationships are evolving or changing over time.

uncovered call Alternative name for *naked call.*

underlying stock The stock on which an option is written.

volatility A measurement of a stock's price movement history and market risk, measured by a comparison between current price and annual price range.

volume The number of shares traded during a specified period, either on an exchange as a whole or in an individual stock. Volume is a technical indicator.

weighted moving average A variation of moving average in which greater weight is given to the latest information, and less weight is given to older information.

working capital The difference between current assets and current liabilities. The availability of cash and assets convertible to cash in the short term to fund operations.

working capital turnover A ratio showing how often working capital is used in and replaced by the generation of sales; to compute, divide sales by working capital.

INDEX